THE SEVEN GIFTS OF
THE SPIRIT OF THE LITURGY

The Seven Gifts of *The Spirit of the Liturgy*

Centennial Perspectives on
Romano Guardini's Landmark Work

Edited by
Christopher Carstens

IGNATIUS PRESS   SAN FRANCISCO

Unless otherwise noted, English translations of papal and conciliar documents have been taken from the Vatican website.

Cover art:
Adoration of the Lamb (detail)
Ghent Altarpiece
Jan van Eyck (c. 1390–1441)
St. Bavo's Cathedral, Ghent, Belgium
Wikimedia Commons

Cover design by Enrique J. Aguilar

ISBN 978-1-62164-406-4 (PB)
ISBN 978-1-64229-148-3 (eBook)
Library of Congress Control Number 2020945757
Printed in the United States of America ∞

CONTENTS

INTRODUCTION

by Christopher Carstens

The Spirit of the Liturgy and Vatican II

Take a minute and answer this question in fifty words or less: *What is the "spirit of the liturgy"?*

How did you do?

If you are like me, you may have found the question rather difficult to address—with (in my case, anyway) a bit of hemming and hawing. But why should this be the case for everyone, and especially for anyone interested in and, more to the point, participating in the sacred liturgy on a regular basis?

Ideally, some essential liturgical features ought to spring easily to mind. The spirit of the liturgy, for example, has universal value. It is a prayer that is accessible and applicable to old and young, oriental and occidental, schooled and uneducated. Its universal relevance results from its celebration and manifestation of objective truth, a feature that allows entire bodies of the faithful—along with the entire Body of the Faithful—to engage in an immensely corporate action. The liturgy's spirit finds sensible expression in sacramental symbols, a medium meant to express both beauty and seriousness—for salvation in Christ is both. And while salvation, adoration, and divination are the most meaningful realities, they are otherwise purposeless and without any practical use beyond themselves. Indeed, knowing and loving the truth, regardless of how it stirs us into action, occupies a central place in the spirit of the liturgy.

The above-named characteristics of the spirit of the liturgy are treated in Romano Guardini's 1918 book, *The Spirit of the Liturgy*. One of the twentieth-century liturgical movement's founding texts, its influence—as one theological expert at the Second Vatican Council put it—was decisive. Indeed, the Fathers of the Second Vatican Council (1962–1965) seemed to have had a clear "spirit of the liturgy" in mind, for they used the phrase regularly in the Constitution on the Sacred Liturgy, *Sacrosanctum concilium*. For example, fostering the laity's active participation—that "aim to be considered before all else" (14)—will be impossible to achieve "unless the pastors themselves, in the first place, become thoroughly imbued with *the spirit and power of the liturgy*" (14, emphasis added).

But the Council Fathers were not only intent on fostering this spirit in their own generation—they sought out the rising generation of priests as well. Since, then, the seeds of sound pastoral practice— especially with regard to the liturgy—sprout in the seminary, the constitution directs that seminarians "celebrate the sacred mysteries, as well as popular devotions which are imbued with the *spirit of the liturgy*" (17, emphasis added). In fact, the entire seminary atmosphere ought to "be thoroughly influenced by the *spirit of the liturgy*" (ibid., emphasis added).

Additionally, liturgical ministers "must all be deeply imbued with *the spirit of the liturgy*" (29, emphasis added). Elements from secular culture may be incorporated "into the liturgy itself", the Fathers allowed, but only "so long as they harmonize with its *true and authentic spirit*" (37, emphasis added). Likewise, musical styles besides Gregorian chant can be sung in the liturgy "so long as they accord with *the spirit of the liturgical action*" (116, emphasis added), and sacred artists themselves are to be imbued "with *the spirit of sacred art and of the sacred liturgy*" (127, emphasis added).

In short: the "spirit of the liturgy" moves throughout the text of *Sacrosanctum concilium*. We might even say that it *inspires* this foremost liturgical document of the Second Vatican Council. But the question posed at the outset—What *is* the spirit of the liturgy?—still needs further precision, especially if we wish to read the Constitution on the Sacred Liturgy properly and catch the liturgical spirit fully today. We must look, therefore, inside the minds of the Council Fathers. Or, better put, look *behind* them to the twentieth-century liturgical movement that preceded the council's work.

Searching for the Source of the Spirit

The expression "spirit of the liturgy" makes an important appearance in at least two preconciliar documents—one from Pius XII and one from his immediate predecessor, Pius XI. In the Church's first encyclical entirely devoted to the sacred liturgy, *Mediator Dei* (1947), Pope Pius XII (1939–1958) spoke to the heart of the matter when encouraging the faithful, "in keeping with *the spirit of the sacred liturgy*, [to] be most closely united with the High Priest and His earthly minister, at the time the consecration of the divine Victim is enacted" (104, emphasis added). Later in the text, after discussing the laudable thanksgiving after receiving Jesus in Holy Communion, Pius XII cites Thomas à Kempis' *The Imitation of Christ*, which says: "Remain on in secret and take delight in your God; for He is yours whom the whole world cannot take away from you." This advice, Pius XII says, "speaks in accordance with the letter and *the spirit of the liturgy*" (126, emphasis added).

Pope Pius XI (1922–1939) also saw this spirit emanating from the liturgy when he was writing *Divini cultus*, his document recalling the twenty-fifth anniversary of *Tra le sollecitudini*, Pope Pius X's 1903 magna carta for the liturgical movement. In *Divini cultus*, Pius XI suggests that seminarians will find relief from their academic studies by learning about or singing Gregorian chant if "carried out in *the spirit of the Liturgy*".

And why should they not? For the Church's treasures of sacred music are the exterior fruit of her interior life of prayer and have been "handed down to posterity, imbued as they were with pious zeal and with *the spirit of the Liturgy*" (ibid., emphases added).

But even these documents have a predecessor, and they emerge from one of the liturgical movement's bedrocks: Romano Guardini's 1918 work, *The Spirit of the Liturgy*. To understand better how even these papal documents, and eventually *Sacrosanctum concilium*, find their theological and historical bearings in Guardini, it is important to know who Guardini was and how he became the liturgical lodestar for popes and Council Fathers alike.

Guardini's The Spirit of the Liturgy

Romano Guardini was born in Verona, Italy, in 1885, but his family quickly moved to Mainz, Germany, where he spent most of his youth. His early education revealed him to be something of a polymath, as he studied both chemistry and economics before hearing the call of the priesthood. Following his ordination to the priesthood in 1910, Guardini put aside molecule charts and inflation bar charts to focus on the writings of Saint Bonaventure and especially his teaching on salvation. But Guardini was no pointy-headed intellectual secluded in an ivory tower—he learned the pastoral side of the priesthood in the most grueling circumstances of his age, serving as a hospital orderly during World War I. After the war, though, he returned to the lecture halls of his early priesthood as a university professor. But even here, he took up a difficult pastoral challenge, devoting much of his energy to working outside of the classroom—in this case, it was a *castle*—with many of his students. At Burg Rothenfels, Guardini and his students took up cultural questions, debated social renewal, and celebrated the liturgy together. Thus, Guardini's education and pastoral practice provided a many-sided view of the world of man, the world of faith, and the spirit enlivening both.

Guardini also had time outside of his university work to undertake his true passion—the liturgy. He was a collaborator with key figures of the liturgical movement from the Benedictine monastery of Maria Laach, in western Germany. With Dom Odo Casel (1886–1948), whose "Mystery Theology" (*Mysterientheologie*) Joseph Ratzinger called "perhaps the most fruitful theological idea of our century",[1] Guardini coedited fifteen volumes of a journal of "liturgical science" (*Jahrbuch fur Liturgiewissenshcaft*) from 1921–1941. One of the most important efforts of Guardini's association with Maria Laach came to fruition in 1918.

---

[1] Joseph Ratzinger, *Collected Works*, vol. 11, ed. Michael J. Miller, trans. John Saward et al., *Theology of the Liturgy* (San Francisco: Ignatius Press, 2014), 153.

That year, Maria Laach's abbot, Ildenfons Herwegen, published Guardini's *The Spirit of the Liturgy* in the first volume of the abbey's *Ecclesia Orans* series.[2]

More than eighty years after the publication of Guardini's text, Joseph Ratzinger would claim that *The Spirit of the Liturgy* "may rightly be said to have inaugurated the Liturgical Movement in Germany. Its contribution was decisive. It helped us to rediscover the liturgy in all its beauty, hidden wealth, and time-transcending grandeur, to see it as the animating center of the Church, the very center of Christian life."[3] What "animated" the liturgy—or, rather, what animated the Church's vision and liturgical apostolate—were Guardini's principal insights spread over *The Spirit of the Liturgy*'s seven short but densely informative chapters. These chapters and the spirit they sought to capture are the purpose and scope of the present book. For the book that Guardini wrote in 1918 remains, one hundred years later, a work that increases in value—not only in its historical importance for the Second Vatican Council, but also for its insights into the twenty-first-century state of affairs regarding the liturgical reform called for by the council.

---

[2] Joseph Cardinal Ratzinger, *The Spirit of the Liturgy*, trans. John Saward (2000), in Joseph Cardinal Ratzinger, *The Spirit of the Liturgy*, with Romano Guardini, *The Spirit of the Liturgy*, Commemorative edition (San Francisco: Ignatius Press, 2018), 21.

[3] Ibid.

The Spirit Is Willing

In 2018, *Adoremus Bulletin* celebrated the centenary of Guardini's spiritual insights with reflections on each of his seven chapters. If the Fathers from the Second Vatican Council felt the "spirit of the liturgy" animating so many liturgical realities, and if their understanding of that "spirit of the liturgy" was instilled in them by the twentieth century's liturgical movement in general and Romano Guardini's *The Spirit of the Liturgy* in particular, then today's own liturgical celebrations, appreciation, and prayer ought also to come to life by the same "spirit".

An Objective Spirit

The Spirit of the Liturgy's first chapter is ostensibly about the "prayer of the liturgy", as its title indicates. But underlying liturgical prayer is a more fundamental truth, namely, that the liturgy is an act of the Mystical Body of Christ—not a series of subjective acts reducible to the individuals who compose them. Bishop Arthur Serratelli of Paterson, New Jersey, has served as chair of the USCCB's Committee on Divine Worship and as a member of three authoritative liturgical bodies: the Congregation for Divine Worship and the Discipline of the Sacraments, the International Commission on English in the Liturgy, and the Holy See's Vox Clara Commission. Writing for *Adoremus*

(January 2018), he summarizes Guardini's principal point this way: "the liturgy is the prayer of the whole Church. It does not rest with the individual nor with a particular community or group of individuals." In fact, the Mystical Body's prayer must be so, Guardini observes, for it is "composed of people of highly varied circumstances, drawn from distinct social strata, perhaps even from different races, in the course of different historical and cultural periods". Consequently, "the ephemeral, adventitious, and locally characteristic elements are, to a certain extent, eliminated, and that which is universally accepted as binding and essential comes to the fore. In other words, the canon of spiritual administration becomes, in the course of time, objective and impartial. The Catholic liturgy is the supreme example of an objectively established rule of spiritual life."[4] Devotions and private prayer, on the other hand, are often as unique and subjective as those who pray them. Characteristic of liturgy's corporate, objective prayer is its close association with dogma, truth, thought, and simplicity of language. And while all other forms of non-liturgical prayer also ought to be true and dogmatic, these latter forms are allowed to express one's individual language, desires, needs, and tastes. In short, the spirit of liturgical prayer is objective, not subjective.

[4] Romano Guardini, *The Spirit of the Liturgy*, trans. Ada Lane (1998), in Ratzinger, *Spirit of the Liturgy*, 276–77.

A Corporate Spirit

Related to the spirit of the liturgy's objective character is its corporate one. The liturgy emphasizes the objective over the subjective because it is first and foremost an action of the larger Church rather than of her particular members. Truly, as far as the spirit of liturgical prayer is concerned, the whole is greater than the sum of its parts. The author of the second essay in this book, Cassian Folsom, O.S.B., is a teacher of liturgy at the Pontifical Liturgical Institute in Rome and founder and prior emeritus of the Monks of Norcia, Saint Benedict's birthplace. Father Cassian explains that Guardini sees ecclesial fellowship as an essential ingredient in the spirit of the liturgy. When Guardini raises this topic of fellowship, Father Cassian writes, "he is talking about ... the Church, the *corpus Christi mysticum*, the 'we' of the entire body of the Church." The spirit of the liturgy is a corporate one, Father Cassian notes, where individual likes and dislikes, virtues and vices, strengths and weaknesses are set aside for the sake of the larger body. Because the liturgy resists—or should resist—such individualization, the corporate nature of liturgical worship demands that individual Christians bring a spirit of humility to ecclesial prayer. "It is on the plane of liturgical relations", Guardini writes, "that the individual experiences the meaning of religious fellowship. The individual—provided that he actually desires to take part in the celebration of the liturgy—must realize that it is as a member of the

Church that he, and the Church within him, acts and prays; he must know that in this higher unity he is at one with the rest of the faithful, and he must desire to be so."[5]

A Universal Spirit

In Guardini's third chapter, "The Style of the Liturgy", he continues to build upon the objective and corporate features examined in the first two chapters. In seeking to elucidate this style (which is the most difficult chapter in Guardini's book), Dr. Michon Matthiesen, Associate Professor at the University of Mary, Bismarck, North Dakota, begins with a question: "Does the liturgy *have* a particular kind of style? Has the public worship of the Church, over the course of the centuries, developed *a* style, a *modus operandi* that best suits ... the praise of God and the sanctification of his people? Guardini undoubtedly believes this to be the case." While any system of thought, any masterpiece of art, or monument may be rightly said to have a particular "style", not all styles appear as grand and universal as others. To the degree that the work—Guardini compares the examples of a Greek temple and the Gothic cathedral—retains its particular time-bound and location-specific features, the universal style is mired in these details. One of Guardini's illustrations is the Gothic cathedral at Cologne: while

[5] Ibid., 299.

this church exemplifies the Gothic style everywhere, it still retains, to a particular degree, the individual character of fourteenth-century France. But when the universal truth transcends the work's specific temporal and cultural features, as in the Paestum Temple of the ancient Greek design, its style is more universal in scope—less time-bound and relative—and is consequently able to speak more powerfully and clearly to men and women in all times and places. The liturgy, says Guardini, possesses (or should possess) style in this latter, more universal sense, one rising above the particularities of the group's uniqueness. "[W]e shall always find, within the sphere of the liturgy, that the medium of spiritual expression, whether it consists of words, gestures, colors, or materials, is to a certain degree divested of its singleness of purpose, intensified, tranquilized, and given universal currency."[6] The spirit of the liturgy is universal, not limited or weakened by particular circumstances. However, the liturgy's universality does not mean it is abstract and inaccessible to the individual.

A Symbolic Spirit

The objective, corporate, and universal spirit of the liturgy becomes concrete in *The Spirit of the Liturgy*'s fourth chapter, "The Symbolism of the Liturgy". But

---

[6] Ibid., 308.

it is not a private or gnostic symbolism that the liturgy employs as a medium. Notre Dame's David Fagerberg puts it succinctly when in his *Adoremus* entry on this symbolism, he writes, "The Lord's Supper did not continue as a Passion Play; it was transformed into a universal currency that could be used in every culture and every century." As Dr. Fagerberg explains, the Last Supper—and, in fact, all that Jesus does to save us—has been turned into a symbol: it has been *symbolized*. For many ears today, Fagerberg notes, "symbol" rings hollow. But for Guardini—and for the Catholic liturgy—symbols are a vital and substantial means by which Jesus and his saving work are manifested to the world today. Sacraments are, after all, a species of symbol: they are sacred and supernatural symbols. As Guardini writes, "A symbol may be said to originate when that which is interior and spiritual finds expression in that which is exterior and material." In fact, "the spiritual element [must] transpose itself into material terms because it is vital and essential that it should do so."[7] Thus, if the liturgy is essentially symbolic, the "people who really live by the liturgy will come to learn that the bodily movements, the actions, and the material objects that it employs are all of the highest significance."[8] The spirit of the liturgy is a symbolic one, where otherwise unseen realities—viz.,

[7] Ibid., 320–21.
[8] Ibid., 324.

Jesus' Paschal Mystery—appear visible (and tasteable, touchable, audible, and smellable) in our midst.

A Meaningful (If Purposeless) Spirit

Chapter 5 of *The Spirit of the Liturgy* bears the title, "The Playfulness of the Liturgy". While the liturgy is not reducible to a mere game, for example, it shares a key feature: both games and liturgies are *without purpose*. But the liturgy's very "purposelessness" fills the spirit of the liturgy with another value: *meaning*. To understand this apparent paradox, pastor of Holy Name Parish in Denver and Benedict XVI Chair for Liturgical Studies at the archdiocese's Saint John Vianney Theological Seminary, Father Daniel Cardó sees "purpose" as "an organizing principle that subordinates actions toward an external goal. Projects and professions are normally organized by their purpose. But there are things in life that are purpose-*less*." But lacking purpose in no way means being void of *meaning*. Quite the contrary. As Guardini writes in the fifth chapter of his book, "The liturgy has no purpose, or, at least, it cannot be considered from the standpoint of purpose. It is not a means that is adapted to attain a certain end—it is an end in itself."[9] Worshipping God, sanctifying oneself by means of his grace, interceding for the salvation of the world: these indeed are

[9] Ibid., 331.

"ends in themselves", not meant for another purpose: and for this very reason, they are full of meaning. "The liturgy", continues Guardini, "creates a universe brimming with fruitful spiritual life and allows the soul to wander about in it at will and to develop itself there."[10] Thus, while we ought to bring any and all of our wants and needs before the Father at the liturgy, each is subsumed under the liturgy's ultimate meaning: God's glory and the world's sanctification. With this meaning, David danced in play before the ark—and with this meaning, Christ stood still on the Cross long enough to die.

A Beautiful Spirit

Even though the liturgical spirit is playful and purposeless, it remains nonetheless serious. As the sixth essayist in this collection, Bishop James Conley of the Diocese of Lincoln, Nebraska, writes, "Liturgy is a serious work—a work of the Lord and a work of the Church—and to serve its sacred and noble purpose, it must be beautiful." In fact, upon first reading, Guardini's penultimate chapter might more accurately be named "The Beauty of the Liturgy". Guardini equates seriousness and beauty based upon their relation to God, who is truth himself. Again, as Bishop Conley says, "Beautiful liturgy does not begin with

[10] Ibid.

the aesthetic preferences of the celebrant. It does not even begin with the treasures of the Church's liturgical tradition. Beautiful liturgy begins with real and intimate union with the Lord." As Guardini would claim, "Those who aspire to a life of beauty must, in the first place, strive to be truthful and good."[11] As for the liturgy, it "must chiefly be regarded from the standpoint of salvation".[12] The goodness, truth, and beauty of salvation: even as these "purposeless" ends reflect the spirit of the liturgy's divine end, they also imbue life with its most serious meaning. Meeting God is serious business, and the liturgy is the means to make this serious project a reality. The spirit of the liturgy is beautiful because it reflects the ultimate end of such beauty for each soul—we sincerely pray—to see God face to face and thereby to encounter beauty unimaginable.

A Logical Spirit

Man is both a thinking and an acting being. And insofar as the liturgy is a true school of human formation— even as it forms us for divine life—the spirit of the liturgy addresses both thought and action. This dual accommodation is the key to understanding the spirit of the liturgy in all its complexity, according to Father

[11] Ibid., 347.
[12] Ibid., 350.

Emery de Gaál, professor of dogmatic theology at the University of Saint Mary of the Lake/Mundelein Seminary. Father Emery asks, "Does the Word or the Deed enjoy pride of place? That is, which is more fundamental in the Christian life: knowledge and truth (*Logos*) or will and action (*Ethos*)?" As his last word on the spirit of the liturgy, Guardini shows in his book's final chapter that the primacy belongs to the Logos: "it must be pointed out that an extensive, biased, and lasting predominance of the will over knowledge is profoundly at variance with the Catholic spirit."[13] Guardini continues: "Truth is truth because it is truth. The attitude of the will to it, and its action toward it, is of itself a matter of indifference to truth."[14] Accordingly, "In the liturgy, the Logos has been assigned its fitting precedence over the will."[15] The spirit of the liturgy, then, is not principally some call to action (even though it does impel us to act), but it is an occasion to meet, reflect upon, and even reflect Truth itself.

Long Live the Spirit of the Liturgy!

Let us pause for a moment and return to the question that began this introduction: *What is the "spirit of*

---

[13] Ibid., 357.
[14] Ibid., 359–60.
[15] Ibid., 363.

the liturgy"? The answer, in seven simple yet loaded words, is that the "spirit of the liturgy" is objective, corporate, universal, symbolic, meaningful, beautiful, and logical. If this was your answer from the outset (I confess that it was not mine when I first began studying the liturgy), then you are not only inhaling the same spirit of the liturgy that Guardini did, but are taking up that same spirit (and are taken up by that same spirit) which moved the Council Fathers to see it as the animating factor in the Church's liturgical life. As noted above, Joseph Ratzinger describes *The Spirit of the Liturgy* as a trailblazing document in the years after its publication: "It led to a striving for a celebration of the liturgy that would be 'more substantial'.... We were now willing to see the liturgy—in its inner demands and form—as the prayer of the Church, a prayer moved and guided by the Holy Spirit himself, a prayer in which Christ unceasingly becomes contemporary with us, enters into our lives."[16]

But what Guardini's masterpiece was doing after 1918, we should still be witnessing after its 2018 centenary. But naming seven descriptors of the spirit of the liturgy does not equate to explaining them or seeing why the liturgy ought to be characterized by them. Indeed, since the 1963 promulgation of *Sacrosanctum concilium*, many have not seen "the spirit of the liturgy" as Guardini and the Council Fathers did.

[16]Ratzinger, *Spirit of the Liturgy*, 21.

For this reason, we have also included as an afterword a masterful summary by Susan Benofy discussing how a pseudo-spirit of the liturgy began to blow in the intervening years. Indeed, too few souls share Guardini's and the council's spirit today. Many liturgies are characterized by subjectivism and individualism rather than by an objective and corporate spirit. Oftentimes, liturgies are custom made, lacking the universal spirit. It is common practice for liturgies to include frivolous and anemic symbols, rather than robust and substantial symbols that truly manifest Christ. Regularly, too, liturgies lack beauty—and seriousness. Too many liturgies weaken our encounter with the Truth and, instead, seek to move our wills and our actions independently from the truth.

We hamper the spirit of the liturgy if we do not know what it is, if we do not desire it, and if we do not work to let it animate liturgical prayer and practice. For these reasons, Romano Guardini's *The Spirit of the Liturgy* and, we hope, Adoremus' own *The Seven Gifts of* The Spirit of the Liturgy will remain insightful books well into the future.

Chapter I

The Prayer of the Liturgy

How the Spirit's Sober
Inebriation Brings Joy
to the Praying Soul

Bishop Arthur J. Serratelli

Romano Guardini is one of the most important intellectual figures in twentieth-century Catholicism. In an era when the Church was facing Modernism and a very individualistic understanding of prayer, Guardini spoke about the liturgy as a communal act of worship of the whole Church. In the nineteenth century, there had been an overemphasis on personal prayer as a means to gain merit and assure one's salvation. To such a spiritual individualism, Guardini provided the much-needed antidote in his famous work *The Spirit of the Liturgy* (1918).

Beyond the Letter

Guardini found little comfort in the textbook theology taught in his day as a defense against the errors of the Modernists. He turned to the writings of Saint Augustine in the quest to uncover the meaning of love and freedom. Guardini realized that there is no true freedom apart from the authority of the Church. His quest for such freedom drew him into the beginnings of the liturgical movement that served as a basis for the Second Vatican Council's renewal of the liturgy. He wanted to relearn the way in which liturgy should be done so that the faithful of his day could more fully enter into it. Long before the Second Vatican Council clearly stated it, Guardini was working for the full, conscious, active participation of all the faithful in liturgy.

So important had the question of the liturgy become in the nineteenth and twentieth centuries that the Second Vatican Council dedicated its first document to the liturgy: *Sacrosanctum concilium*. In the early twentieth century, Pope Saint Pius X had sought to encourage a more active participation of the laity at Mass through a reform of liturgical music. Subsequently, in response to the liturgical movement taking place, Pope Pius XII had issued *Mediator Dei* in 1947. It was the very first encyclical devoted entirely to the liturgy. In it, Pope Pius XII defined the liturgy as "the public worship ... rendered by the Mystical Body of Christ in the entirety of its Head and members".[1] He encouraged the active participation of the laity in the Mass and spoke of the liturgy as a source for personal piety.

At the very beginning of this growing desire for a liturgical revival, Guardini published his book *The Spirit of the Liturgy*. Although it was published a century ago, it remains a powerful statement of the true nature of the liturgy. "In his classic *The Spirit of the Liturgy*, Guardini presented the experience of the liturgy as an antidote to the cold rationalism and narrow moralism that he saw afflicting the Church of his day."[2]

Guardini's profound insights have not been surpassed. They continue to engage theologians. In writing his own masterpiece on the liturgy, Cardinal Ratzinger used the same title for his work as Guardini did, and he humbly acknowledged his own indebtedness to Guardini. Both authors set as their purpose, not simply to debate scholarly questions, but to offer an understanding of how faith finds its expression in the celebration of the liturgy.

Prayer—One and All

In the first chapter of his book, "The Prayer of the Liturgy", Guardini discusses the relationship between

---

[1] Pius XII, Encyclical *Mediator Dei* on the Sacred Liturgy (November 20, 1947), 20.

[2] Christopher Shannon, "Romano Guardini: Father of the New Evangelization", *Crisis*, February 17, 2014.

liturgy and popular devotions as well as the relevance of culture for liturgy. He begins by establishing the principle that the liturgy is the prayer of the whole Church. It does not rest with the individual or with a particular community or group of individuals. In fact, the liturgy's first aim is not the awakening of the pious sentiments of an individual or a community. For Guardini, the objective nature of the liturgy is fundamental. It is what distinguishes Catholic worship and sets it apart from Protestant worship, which is much more subjective and individualistic.

The Church is all-embracing, including people of every race, distinct social strata, and varied circumstances. In the course of time, her liturgy has developed. The ephemeral, the experimental, and those aspects peculiar to a time or place have been gradually eliminated, and what is accepted as essential and binding on all has remained. "The Catholic liturgy is the supreme example of an objectively established rule of spiritual life. It has been able to develop 'κατὰ τὸν ὅλον, that is to say, in every direction and in accordance with all places, times, and types of human culture".[3]

Guardini's insistence on the objective nature of the liturgy provides an ever-present safeguard against attitudes and actions that undermine the liturgy. Since the

---

[3] Romano Guardini, *The Spirit of the Liturgy*, trans. Ada Lane (1998), in Joseph Cardinal Ratzinger, *The Spirit of the Liturgy*, with Romano Guardini, *The Spirit of the Liturgy*, Commemorative edition (San Francisco: Ignatius Press, 2018), 277.

liturgy is something that we receive from the Church, it is never the product of a particular group. No individuals or groups of individuals have the prerogative to be creative with the liturgy, adapting, changing, or removing parts of the liturgy to suit their particular subjective perception of what is required at any given moment.

Developing this same thought, Ratzinger in his writings and speeches urges Catholics to have a new awareness of the liturgy as a gift received from the Church. Such an understanding does not reduce the liturgy to something that can be manipulated at will. When individuals reshape the liturgy to project their own will and desires, they lose its primary focus. The liturgy is not to make us feel good. Perhaps, such thinking is one factor among others that accounts for the decrease in attendance at the liturgy in the last fifty years. Liturgy is not me-centered: it is God-centered.

Side by side with the universal, objective, and public liturgy of the Church are the private prayers of her individual members. In these private prayers and communal devotions of the faithful, there is a stronger presence of emotion and feeling. Popular piety is personal and subjective. Its forms vary according to historical circumstances, "periods, localities, or requirements, and so on. They bear the stamp of their time and surroundings and are the direct expression of the characteristic quality or temper of an individual congregation."[4] Nevertheless, these acts of piety contribute in their own way to the spiritual growth of the individual. They are necessary and good.

Guardini is balanced in his discussion of prayer. Both the private prayer of the faithful and the public prayer of the Church foster and deepen a person's relationship with God. In both personal prayer and devotional prayer, individuals bring to God the particular contingencies and needs of their lives. In the liturgy, however, individuals are absorbed into a wider spiritual world and pray as members of the Church. They are taken up into a sphere that transcends the individual and is accessible to believers of every time and place. Both popular devotions and the public worship of the Church have their place. "There could be no greater mistake", Guardini insists, "than that of discarding the valuable elements in the spiritual life of the people for the sake of the liturgy, or than the desire of assimilating them to it."[5]

Nonetheless, liturgical prayer has a preeminence over non-liturgical prayer. Examining what a healthy relationship between liturgical prayer and devotional prayer looks like, Guardini extrapolates a number of "fundamental laws"[6] from the liturgy that ought to guide a necessary, healthy, and supporting piety.

[4] Ibid., 278.
[5] Ibid., 279.
[6] Ibid.

Liturgical Laws

The first two laws involve the head and the heart—
thought and emotion. Since prayer is always the lift-
ing up of our hearts to God, emotions will always
have their place in every form of prayer. But, in popular devotions, there may be an emphasis on a specific
emotion or form of spontaneity that may not elicit a
response in all present and may not be reproduced at
every occasion. Liturgy, on the other hand, is more
universal and inclusive.

The heart must be in all prayer. And, in the liturgy,
the heart is guided and purified by the mind. Feeling
and emotion are present, but thought directs and con-
trols them. "If prayer in common", Guardini says, "is
to prove beneficial to the majority, it must be primarily directed by thought, and not by feeling."[7] Clear
theological thought sustains and directs the prayers
of the liturgy. It is precisely this direction that makes
liturgical prayer helpful for the entire community.

Related to the law of the mind is the foundational
element of truth. Prayer, whether liturgical or devotional, "is beneficial only when it rests on the bedrock
of truth".[8] The very words of the prayers of the liturgy
are taken from the rich storehouse of Sacred Scripture
and tradition. The words of the Fathers of the Church

[7] Ibid., 281.
[8] Ibid.

find their voice in the liturgy. In the carefully con-
structed phrases of the liturgical prayer, the faith of the
entire Church across the centuries is expressed both
artistically and didactically. Unlike popular devotions,
the liturgy does not concentrate our attention on one
truth to the exclusion of another. For example, the
mercy of God is never emphasized to the detriment
of the justice of God or the transcendence of God to
his immanence.

In lucid terms, the liturgy, guided by dogma, offers
the truth of the faith in its entirety. In this way, the
liturgy not only teaches us, but satisfies our deepest
spiritual hunger. In a word, the liturgy "is nothing
else but truth expressed in terms of prayer".[9] As Guardini so beautifully writes, "Dogmatic thought brings
release from the thraldom of individual caprice and
from the uncertainty and sluggishness that follow in
the wake of emotion. It makes prayer intelligible and
causes it to rank as a potent factor in life."[10]

But that is not to say that emotions and feelings do
not play their part in the liturgy. "While the necessity of thought is emphasized," Guardini explains, "it
must not be allowed to degenerate into the mere frigid
domination of reason."[11] The emotional element of
prayer is another law accompanying prayer's truth
feature. Our human nature is both graced and fallen,

[9] Ibid., 283.
[10] Ibid., 282.
[11] Ibid., 284.

splendid and base. In the liturgy, all the emotions of our common human nature are present from A to Z. The intense cries of the psalmist's voice convey both our joys and our sorrows. The plaintive sighs of the *Miserere*—"Have mercy on me, O God, according to your merciful love!" (Ps 51:1)—express our deep contrition. The Easter *Exsultet* raises our hearts in joyful praise of God, who brings to fulfillment his plan of salvation in the Resurrection of Jesus. In the liturgy, emotion is always controlled and tranquil. "Emotion glows in its depths, but it smolders merely, like the fiery heart of the volcano, whose summit stands out clear and serene against the quiet sky."[12]

Digging Deep

Lastly, in his first chapter of *The Spirit of the Liturgy*, Guardini goes beneath the surface of prayer. He speaks of the "great ... need of the subsoil of healthy nature".[13] An individual's human nature, along with a society's corporate nature, is part and parcel of a healthy and vibrant life of prayer. He holds that, like the salt of the gospel, a genuine and lofty culture should impregnate the entire spiritual life. Without a lofty culture, ideas become weak, symbolism crude,

[12] Ibid., 285.
[13] Ibid., 294.

and language coarse. Guardini often employs the Scholastic maxim, "grace takes nature for granted."[14] When a natural foundation is strong and solid, a supernatural edifice may rise toward God; conversely, when the footing is faulty, divine life is difficult—if not impossible. Since human culture influences the spiritual life, by that very fact, it influences liturgy.

Most certainly, culture, especially the use of language, is important in liturgy. As Pope Benedict XVI stated in his book, *The Spirit of the Liturgy*: "This action of God, which takes place through human speech, is the real 'action' for which all creation is in expectation.... This is what is new and distinctive about the Christian liturgy: God himself acts and does what is essential."[15] Since the language of liturgical prayer is so essential to presenting the "action" of God, it deserves special attention. "Coarse language" and "monotonous and clumsy imagery" are simply not capable of communicating clearly the *actio* of the Divine Word.

In the liturgy, the language of prayer should be rich in thought and imagery. It must not be removed from reality—it should be bold enough to call things by their names. It should be powerful, yet subtle. It should be erudite, yet understandable.

Liturgical prayer should tend toward the poetic. While prose bumps along the ground, poetry reaches

---

[14] Ibid.

[15] Joseph Ratzinger, *The Spirit of the Liturgy*, trans. John Saward (2000), in Ratzinger, *Spirit of the Liturgy*, 187.

heavenward. And liturgy already participates in the liturgy of heaven.[16] "If indeed, in the liturgical texts, words or expressions are sometimes employed which differ somewhat from usual and everyday speech, it is often enough by virtue of this very fact that the texts become truly memorable and capable of expressing heavenly realities."[17]

Even a casual reader of the first chapter of Guardini's *The Spirit of the Liturgy* comes quickly to a basic understanding of Catholic liturgy as "the supreme example of an objectively established rule of spiritual life".[18] As Prosper of Aquitaine's maxim *lex orandi, lex credendi* succinctly expresses, the liturgy is our teacher. It contains "the entire body of religious truth".[19] It is the treasure-house of the truths of revelation; indeed, the content of liturgical prayer is the Word himself. Liturgical prayer is truly the font and summit of the Christian life (cf. *Lumen gentium*, 11), for in it Christ becomes (as Cardinal Ratzinger would put it) "contemporary with us [and] enters into our lives".[20]

---

[16] See Arthur Serratelli, "Liturgy Language: Soaring Poetry vs. Bumpy Prose", *Zenit*, June 19, 2008, https://www.zenit.org/articles/liturgy-language-soaring-poetry-vs-bumpy-prose/.

[17] Congregation for Divine Worship and the Discipline of the Sacraments, Instruction *Liturgiam authenticam* on the Use of Vernacular Languages in the Publication of the Books of the Roman Liturgy (March 28, 2001), 27.

[18] Guardini, *Spirit of the Liturgy*, 277.

[19] Ibid., 283.

[20] Ratzinger, *Spirit of the Liturgy*, 21.

Chapter II

The Fellowship of the Liturgy

Each for All and All for Christ

Cassian Folsom, O.S.B.

The philosophical writings of Romano Guardini on the relationship of the individual to the community are like a luxurious vine: trunk, branches, tendrils extending here and there, leaves and, of course, fruit in abundance. In this article, the reader will get a stripped-down version, reduced to the essentials, and poor in comparison. The hope is that this simplified explanation of Guardini's thought will lead the reader to the text itself, *The Spirit of the Liturgy*, where he can enjoy the full breadth of our author's insights.

First a summary of chapter 2, "The Fellowship of the Liturgy", will be given. Next, the ideas presented in this chapter will be fleshed out by insights from other works of Guardini. Finally, there will be a reflection on the implications of Guardini's thought for liturgical reform.

Summing up "Fellowship"

Guardini's philosophical musings are rich and densely packed. In this second chapter of *The Spirit of the Liturgy*, it might be helpful to use the interpretive key of participation, although Guardini does not use the word here. He explains that the liturgical fellowship, or *Gemeinschaft*, he is talking about is the Church, the *corpus Christi mysticum*, the "we" of the entire body of the Church. How does the individual "I" relate to this liturgical community? Or, in other words, how do I participate in the Church's liturgy? Let us examine the following elements more closely: (A) the community, (B) the individual, and (C) the participation of the individual in the liturgical action of the community.

A. The Community[1]

The liturgy is celebrated, not by the individual, but by the entire body of the faithful, not merely those present, but all the faithful on earth (across the limits of time and space) and all the saints in heaven. "Who

[1] This is a summary and paraphrase of Romano Guardini, *The Spirit of the Liturgy*, trans. Ada Lane (1998), in Joseph Cardinal Ratzinger, *The Spirit of the Liturgy*, with Romano Guardini, *The Spirit of the Liturgy*, Commemorative edition (San Francisco: Ignatius Press, 2018), 297ff.

celebrates the liturgy?" In answer to this question, Guardini says: the Church, who is more than the sum of her parts. It is the Mystical Body of Christ, animated by the Holy Spirit. The individual participates in this common action of the Church. In the liturgy, the individual "sees himself face to face with God, not as [a single] entity, but as a member of this unity".[2]

How does the individual person enter into this larger reality of the liturgical community? He does so in two ways: by sacrifice (*Opfer*) and by personal action (*Leistung*).[3] The sacrifice required by the person who wishes to participate in the liturgical fellowship is the renunciation "of everything in him that exists merely for itself and excludes others".[4] The personal action required of him is the widening of his outlook, which results from his acceptance and assimilation of a more comprehensive scheme of life than his own—that of the community.

B. The Individual[5]

Thus we have the big picture: the participation of the individual believer in the common action of the

[2] Ibid., 298.

[3] *Leistung* is very hard to translate. Ada Lane uses a helpful paraphrase: "producing something". The word can mean performance, production, achievement, contribution, work accomplished, etc. In this context, it involves personal action or the acceptance of responsibility as a prerequisite for participating in the common action.

[4] Guardini, *Spirit of the Liturgy*, 299.

[5] This is a summary and paraphrase of Guardini, *Spirit of the Liturgy*, 299–30.

liturgical community. Guardini then examines in greater detail how integration of the individual into the community works. People are not all the same, and therefore their modes of participation in the *Gemeinschaft*, the Mystical Body, will necessarily be different. Guardini takes into consideration two basic temperaments or dispositions: the individualistic disposition (we might say introverted) and the social disposition (we might say extroverted). Within the individualistic category, there is a further subdivision: those drawn to the objective and impersonal and those drawn to the subjective and personal. Thus Guardini speaks of three personality types (to use contemporary language), and for each one, he outlines the kind of asceticism needed (involving sacrifice and personal action) in order to participate in the liturgical community.

The person with an *individualistic temperament, drawn to objective and impersonal thinking*, is concerned with ideas, the ordering of things, objectives, laws, rules, tasks to be accomplished, rights, and duties. He perceives the community as a great concrete order. The *sacrifice* he must make, in order to participate in liturgical fellowship, is to renounce his own ideas and his own spiritual preferences, to submit to the ideas of the liturgy, to surrender his independence and pray with others, to obey the liturgical norms instead of freely disposing of himself, to stand in the ranks. He must take certain forms of *personal action*: shaking off the narrow trammels of his own thought to make way for a far more comprehensive world of ideas, going beyond his personal aims and adopting the aims of the great fellowship of the liturgy, taking part in exercises that do not respond to his particular conscious needs, petitioning God for things that do not directly concern him but concern the community at large, taking part at times in proceedings whose significance he does not entirely understand. The *virtue* required by this kind of person is humility, because he must renounce self-rule and self-sufficiency, accept the principles of the liturgy, overcome pride and intolerance, and assimilate an entire system of communal aims and ideas.

The person with an *individualistic temperament, drawn to subjective expression and feeling,* focuses on his sentiments and intimate feelings. He perceives the community as a broad fabric of personal affinities and interwoven reciprocal relationships. The *sacrifice* he must make in order to participate in liturgical fellowship is to renounce his spiritual isolation, to share his existence with other people, to share with others the intimacy of his inner life and feelings—these others being, not just a few neighbors or congenial friends, but all, even those who are indifferent, adverse, or even hostile. He must take certain forms of *personal action*, for the sensitive soul must break down the barriers around its spiritual life and issue forth from the self in order to go among others and share their existence. The *virtue* required by this kind of person is charity, because he needs that great and wonderful love which is ready to participate in the life of others, that vigorous expansion which goes out of self in order to include others, that life lived in common with the other members of Christ's Body. He must master the repulsion of the strangeness of corporate life and triumph over exclusiveness, that is, the desire to be only with people of his own choosing.

The person with a *social temperament* eagerly and consistently craves for fellowship, automatically seeks out congenial associates, presses toward togetherness in a way alien to the liturgy. People like this will not find all their expectations immediately fulfilled in the liturgy, and the fellowship of the liturgy will appear to them frigid and restricted. The *sacrifice* this kind of person must make in order to participate in liturgical fellowship is different from the other cases. He must accept the boundaries the liturgy imposes on together-ness. He must realize that in the liturgy, the union of the members is not directly accomplished from one person to another, but is accomplished by and in their joint aim, goal, and spiritual resting place—God. In the liturgy, the individual is never drawn into contacts that are too extensively direct, and therefore he must submit to the austere restraint that characterizes litur-gical fellowship. The social temperament must take certain forms of *personal action*. He must realize that in the liturgy, all are not equal, but there are differences of rank and role. The formality of the liturgy pro-duces a certain restraint, a reciprocal reverence. While the liturgy establishes a genuine community, one individual can never force his way into the intimacy of another or force his own characteristics, feelings, and perceptions on the rest of the assembly. He must learn to subscribe to the noble, restrained forms that etiquette requires in the House and at the Court of the Divine Majesty. The *virtue* required by this kind of person is reserve or restraint. It is this reserve alone that in the end makes fellowship in the liturgy possible; but for it, togetherness would be unendurable.

C. Individual Participation in the Liturgical Action of the Community

Thus, in a few short pages, Guardini sketches out for us his understanding of liturgical fellowship, or community, into which individual believers must be inserted. The participation of the individual in the liturgical action of the community requires asceticism, the precise form of which varies considerably from one temperament to another. The common principle, however, is this: the individual must submit himself to the objective order of liturgical prayer.

Guardini on Guardini

In his book, *Liturgical Formation*,[6] written in 1923—a few years after *The Spirit of the Liturgy*—Guardini

---

[6] Original text: Romano Guardini, *Liturgische Bildung. Versuche,* 1923. I am translating from the German edition, *Liturgie und liturgische Bildung* (Mainz: Matthias-Grünewald-Verlag, 1992), and the Italian edition, *Formazione liturgica* (Milan: Edizioni O.R., 1988).

returns to the theme of the relation between the individual and the liturgical community. In brief, he argues that the *whole* man must participate in the *whole* Church in a way that unites the subjective and objective aspects of the human person.

A. The Community[7]

Against what he calls an "anti-historical, rationalistic-doctrinaire and romantic-sentimental" view of the Church, expressed in a false kind of universalism, Guardini insists that the whole Church is incarnate in the diocese and in the local parish. There is no contrast between the Church Universal and the local expression of the Church. Certainly we must understand the Church as a *whole*, since she is founded by Christ and is united in him, "but we must affirm her, love her, live in her and work there where she meets us in an immediate way: in the diocese and in the parish community."[8] The "whole" Church includes both her universal and her particular expressions, both the spiritual reality of the Mystical Body of Christ and the human reality of the hierarchical structure.

---

[7] This is a summary and paraphrase of *Formazione liturgica*, chap. 4, "The Individual and the Community", 61–76.

[8] Ibid., 63.

B. The Individual[9]

Likewise, the individual subject must not be considered in a reductive way. The subject of liturgical behavior is the "whole" man, who includes in his own expression the entire creation. But when is it, Guardini asks, that one can speak of the "whole" man? Only when he is inserted into the community. In both—the totality of the single individual and the totality of the community—there is present something that is beyond time and history. The two things are correlated: the person is oriented toward the vastness of the great human community, which in its turn, however, is composed of individuals who sustain and complete it. In the religious field, he goes on to say, this relationship between individual and community indicates that a complete Christian humanity exists only where the Church and the individual person live in a natural reciprocal relationship. In a way reminiscent of Saint Augustine's expression *Christus totus*, Guardini is arguing for an *Ecclesia tota* and a *homo totus*.[10]

Homo totus includes two forms of liturgical expressivity: the subjective manifestation of personal experience and emotion and the objective emphasis on content, reality, truth, being. In chapter 5 of *Liturgical Formation*, Guardini explores these two aspects

[9] Using material from chapter 4, this section is a summary and paraphrase of *Formazione liturgica*, chapter 5, "The Objective Quality of the Liturgy", 77–100.

[10] These are my terms, not Guardini's.

at length. In the historical context of the time, at the very beginning of the liturgical movement, it was common enough for the objective celebration of the liturgy to go one way, and the subjective piety of the people to go another. Guardini decries this situation in no uncertain terms, lamenting that the profound, authentic *homo liturgicus* has been buried and needs to be awakened. He offers a severe critique of an excessively subjective liturgical piety.

This critique is worth summarizing here, as our own times are dominated by a similar subjective emphasis. Guardini observes that self-expression, as a manifestation of what is subjective and particular, cannot have any pretense of meaning something to others outside the person or outside the intimate circle of those who are linked to that person. It would be an unbearable presumption, he says, to think that individual self-expression could have any great significance beyond that circle. That which is expressed in this way seduces the community and forces it into a condition in which it becomes an echo of the expressive individual will. This is a form of domination.

On the contrary, Guardini argues for a recovery of the objective meaning of the liturgy. Liturgical expression of this kind is oriented toward otherworldly realities, to metaphysics, to that which endures, and in this way acquires a significance for everyone. This liturgical expression involves also recognizing the laws of the medium of expression (in this case, the liturgy) and having profound respect for them, but inserting these laws into that superior law which allows each element to take its proper place. This kind of liturgical behavior does not dominate, but serves.

While Guardini contrasts the subjective and objective expressions of the individual's behavior in the liturgy, toward the end of his treatment of this topic, he affirms that these two poles of human experience exist together. It becomes a question of in what measure one or the other predominates. Observing things from a historical point of view, Guardini argues that from the Renaissance to the Protestant Reformation all the way to the twentieth century, the subjective aspect has dominated. He sees, in the initial stirrings of the liturgical movement, signs of a return to objectivity.

C. Individual Participation in the Liturgical Action of the Community[11]

In order for the whole man to participate authentically in liturgical fellowship, a rigorous program of liturgical asceticism is necessary. Guardini affirms that the liturgy is the self-expression of man, but of man as he should be (not as he presently is), and, for that reason, the liturgy involves a severe discipline. Liturgical prayer must be accompanied by a long and severe discipline, until the depths of man reawaken. This

[11] This is a summary and paraphrase of *Formazione liturgica*, 90–92.

transformation by means of the liturgy, up until now, can scarcely be found. For that reason, Guardini says, "you must come to my school."[12] We can see that all of his intense philosophical labors were ordered to the goal of liturgical formation.

In 1926, Guardini published an essay about the order that exists between persons.[13] His philosophical reflections on what it means to be a person lie outside our present scope, but suffice it to say that when Guardini insists that the individual must submit himself to the common action of the liturgical community, he does not mean, in any way, to efface the uniqueness of the individual personality. At the end of the essay, he takes up once again the question of the relation of the individual to the larger group. His particular focus in this section is the order that exists between persons. He explains that there is an objective form of order, which exists independently of its individual parts, such as friendship, family, the work group, community, state, and so on. The individual person participates in this objective totality in a way that is free, unconstrained. The unique, unrepeatable person, characterized by self-possession, is connected to the totality in a particular way. That is, the

---

[12] Ibid., 92.

[13] The original text: Romano Guardini, "Über Sozialwissenschaft und Ordnung unter Personen", *Die Schildgenossen* 6 (1926): 125–50. I am using the Italian edition: *Persona e personalità* (Brescia, 2005). This is a summary of section 5: "Order between Persons: Some Distinctions", 62–71.

person not only receives this order, but also *produces* it, and in this way energy and dynamism are released. Herein lies the paradoxical contrast of the relationship between the objective order and the individual person. The impersonal order is based on that which is global, above the person; the individual is drawn into this order willy-nilly. The single person must accept this order, interiorize it, transform it, and then freely externalize it as his own.

Guardini does not apply these natural categories to the Church or to the liturgy; in fact, he says in a note that this can only be done analogously. But it is easy to see how they could be applied to the liturgy. The question is the relation between the sacred, objective order of the liturgy and the personal, individual subject. Guardini intimates that the participation that takes place here (even if he does not use the word) moves in two directions. The person *receives* the sacred order as objective and given and, by interiorizing it, makes that order his own. Then, *producing* a new synthesis, he bestows that back upon the liturgy.

Formulating Principles of Reform

To wrestle with Guardini's arguments, to grapple with his philosophical distinctions, is hard work, but very fruitful. His profound reflections show that the relation between the objective order of the liturgy and the personal subject is what we, today, call participation. In Guardini's day, the problem was that there was no appropriation of the objective content of the liturgy. A wall of incomprehension had arisen between the individual and this objective content, and the faithful, frequently enough, were left with their subjective devotions.

Guardini's solution was "participation by means of formation". Or to be more technical, he argued that the objective content of the liturgy, celebrated by the liturgical community, was to be received by the personal subject, appropriated, interiorized, and reproposed, thus creating a remarkable unity or synergy of participation. He realized, however, that such appropriation required the long, severe discipline (or, in other words, asceticism) of liturgical formation.

In the post-Vatican II era, the solution proposed was much different. Having the same goal of the appropriation by the faithful of the content of the liturgy, the strategy devised was to change the liturgy, to adapt its texts and rites, so as to make the subjective appropriation by the faithful easier. What are some of the results? The subjective has taken over once again: a different kind of subjectivity than the one against which Guardini was fighting, but, nonetheless, subjectivity. The celebration of Mass *versus populum* focuses on the subjective (us), not on the objective (Christ's saving action). The sign of peace, which Guardini described as a "masterly manifestation of restrained and elevated social solidarity"[14] when performed according to the rubrics, has degenerated into an artificial and forced intimacy. The liberty granted to the celebrant by the liturgical books to adapt the rite and insert catechetical comments breeds priestly subjectivity. The liberties taken quite beyond what the liturgical books allow are a manifestation of that creativity which arrogantly presumes to impose its subjective experience upon the community. It would seem that the reform of texts and rites is not the answer.

In a famous letter[15] written in 1964 on the occasion of the Third Liturgical Congress in Mainz, Guardini argues that the problems of liturgical reform are not, in the first place, problems of texts and rites, but rather something more fundamental. "If I see correctly," he says, "the typical man of the nineteenth century was no longer capable of the liturgical act, indeed he no longer knew what it was. For him, liturgical behavior was purely and simply the intimate act of the individual—which then, in the context of the liturgy, assumed the character of public and official solemnity."[16] Here Guardini is arguing for a recovery of a sense of the Body of Christ, of the liturgical community. He is also urging a celebration of the liturgy in which the participants act, not by rote, but with full awareness of its meaning. These are great themes

[14] Guardini, *Spirit of the Liturgy*, 303.
[15] This letter can be found in: *Liturgie und liturgische Bildung*, 9–17.
[16] Ibid., 9.

in the liturgical movement, reacting to problems perceived in the liturgical praxis of the nineteenth century. What about the twentieth and twenty-first centuries, after the liturgical movement, after *Sacrosanctum concilium*, in our own day?

One hundred years after the publication of *The Spirit of the Liturgy*, Guardini's teaching remains an important point of reference. His great contribution to the debate, it seems to me, is to call into question the value of the external reform of texts and rites if the deeper problem of liturgical formation is not addressed.

Chapter III

The Style of the Liturgy

Heaven in a Grain of Incense

Michon M. Matthiesen

Theologian David Tracy once told a lecture hall
filled with master's students a "parable" about the
difference between the workings of a German mind
and those of an American one. He said that when
his German theologian friends land at an airport
in the United States, they place their luggage and
briefcases neatly and orderly in the trunk of the
automobile—be it a taxi cab or rental car. Whereas,
he noted, when his American colleagues travel, they
simply toss their valises into the trunk without a
thought to symmetry, balance, or the careful fit of
the space available before them.

This image returned to my mind while preparing to write on the third chapter ("The Style of
the Liturgy") of Guardini's *The Spirit of the Liturgy*.

Guardini's liturgico-spiritual classic is so neatly organized and arranged that a single piece of it depends for
full comprehension on contiguous parts as well as on
the whole frame. Moreover, this particular chapter
on "style" exemplifies the predilection of his German-
trained, if Italian-born, soul for distinctive order and
fruitful tension (suitcases carefully arranged in a trunk
to remain fixed by their very tensive contiguity).

In chapter 1, Guardini orders the proper balance in
liturgical prayer between thought and emotion and
between nature and civilization. Chapter 2 reveals
the delicate polarity between the individual and the
community in the liturgy. In chapter 3, while explicat-
ing the *style* of the liturgy, Guardini draws attention
to the inherent tension in the liturgy between individual expression and the universal, between historical time and the eternal, and between the warm
ebullience of private devotions and the reserved style
of the Church's public prayer.

Though writing in 1918, as the final battles of the
Great War subsided, Guardini's articulation of what
constitutes the style of the liturgy remains essential and as desperately necessary for the restoration of
the twenty-first-century soul—distracted, enslaved to
time, and appallingly "selfie"-obsessed—as it was for
the shattered, disillusioned souls of the 1920s. Does the
liturgy *have* a particular kind of style? Has the public
worship of the Church, over the course of the centuries, developed *a* style, a *modus operandi* that best

THE STYLE OF THE LITURGY   57

suits—is most *conveniens* to—the praise of God and
the sanctification of his people? Guardini undoubtedly believes this to be the case, and he is persuasive
about the necessity and fruits of such a style.

Unpacking "Style"

To comprehend Guardini's vision of the style of the
liturgy, we first need to grapple with the word itself.
Like Augustine's famous quip about "time" in book XI
of the *Confessions*—we all know what it is until we
need to say what it is—"style", too, is a slippery term
to pin down. We do know that there are styles of
painting (Dutch realism, impressionism) and styles
of writing (the expansive and moral prose of Victo-
rians like Charles Dickens and George Eliot and the
modern minimalistic writing of Ernest Hemingway
and Cormac McCarthy). We are familiar with styles
of preaching—the scholarly exposition, the narrative homily, the evangelical double-edged sword to
the heart. We are even able to note political styles of
leading a country: the dictator; the prudent concilia-
tor; the populist "tweeter". But what *is* style? What
counts for style?

Fortunately, Guardini provides us with a definition—
actually, two definitions.

Guardini speaks of style in a broad sense, and then
he chisels the definition to a narrower meaning. Style

in the first sense obtains when any "vital" principle has found its authentic, true expression.[1] This living principle can be a biological organism, a personality, an artistic production, or even the form of a community or society. Yet, to merit the designation of "style", this particular expression must prove to be of wide importance. That is to say, a truly convincing style will establish something with which others may also identify and engage: it will manifest that which is almost already familiar to others, familiar in the sense that its peculiarity is magnanimously accessible.

This definition might sound terribly paradoxical, but it is at the heart of what Guardini wants to communicate about style. The more *original* and impressive the expression, the more capable it is of revealing its "universal essence", of inviting the soul into its reality. Three examples—a personality, a social body, a work of art—might help to illuminate what Guardini indicates by style in this first sense.

Person, Place, and Poem

The saint is a "genius" personality who has exhibited something "immeasurably original", a highly

---

[1] Romano Guardini, *The Spirit of the Liturgy*, trans. Ada Lane (1998), in Joseph Cardinal Ratzinger, *The Spirit of the Liturgy*, with Romano Guardini, *The Spirit of the Liturgy*, Commemorative edition (San Francisco: Ignatius Press, 2018), 307.

individual style that is not without universal relevancy. Few, for instance, would dispute the originality of Saint Francis: his naked dependence upon God; his compassion for the sick and the poor; his response to rebuild the Church; his love of nature and animals; and his commitment to the way of peace and reconciliation. For almost a thousand years, this particular "Franciscan" style has had a broad appeal, and it has been generative and formative of Christians and non-Christians alike.

Similarly, a form of community can claim a style that is efficacious across time and culture. Saint Benedict's *Rule*, written in sixth-century Italy, established a form of monastic social life dedicated to seeking God (*quaerere Deum*). As Benedict XVI is fond of noting, the *Rule* became a "spiritual leaven" that "changed the face of Europe".[2] The *Rule* would become a template for religious life across the European continent, and today it still stands as a model for religious communities as well as for family and institutional life. The particular Benedictine vision of a school of love, its patterned rhythm of *ora et labora*, and its insistence upon mutual humility and obedience manifests a style that is universally significant and accessible.

Dante's literary masterpiece *La Commedia* also exemplifies Guardini's first notion of style. There is

[2] See, for example, Benedict XVI's General Audience address (April 9, 2008), http://www.vatican.va/content/benedict-xvi/en/audiences/2008/documents/hf_ben-xvi_aud_20080409.html.

no gainsaying that Dante's poem emerges from the very particular historical setting of late medieval Florence. The lengthy and often taxing notes provided by most editors at the end of each canto, detailing historical figures and local Florentine events, remind the reader just how temporally situated the poem is. Even so, the genius of Dante's *Commedia* reaches *through* the particular to the universal. The poet's narrative of a pilgrim's journey through (and to) the afterlife achieves that uniqueness and perfection of expression which makes it also an artwork of universal style. Perhaps unwittingly, the reader finds himself walking in the shoes of Dante's pilgrim.

Each of these instances of style manifests an arc of descending into the finite and particular in order to speak universally. This is the way of our incarnational God, who entered time and history in order to save and raise up fallen creatures. Perhaps all "style", in this first sense, is at best an imitation of this divine arc.

Law and Order

Still, Guardini wishes to refine further his denotation of style—style in a *narrower* sense. It is this second, "specialized meaning" of style that illuminates the nature of the Church's liturgy. Guardini invites his reader to experience this narrow meaning of style through visual imagination.

Place before your eyes an ancient Greek temple and a Gothic cathedral. Both are beautiful; both invoke awe; both are perfect expressions of a particular type that bestows profound insight about a historical period and culture. Guardini leads us to see, however, that the Greek temple has *more* style than the Gothic cathedral.

Alternatively, stand before two equally powerful paintings, one by Giotto and one by Grünewald. Even a person without the advantage of having taken an Art 101 course will see that the Giotto has *more* style—or so Guardini confidently affirms. This "*more*" is precisely what Guardini is after in considering style *in sensu strictu*: this style indicates that the essential and universal assumes ascendency over a distinctive particularity of expression.

We can see in the Paestum Temple and the Giotto painting that what is individual and of time subjects itself to what is essential and transcendent. This narrower understanding of style thus gives precedence to the universal over the historical and concrete. It manifests a simplification of the multiplicity of life, with all its particular "entanglements", by underscoring instead inner coherence, order, and "lawfulness".[3] Just so is the majestic style of the Church's liturgy.

This specialized liturgical style developed organically over time. Guardini argues that the "Greco-Latin

---

[3] Guardini, *Spirit of the Liturgy*, 307.

spirit" (which tends *per se* to this narrower sense of style), the "polishing" and chiseling of liturgical symbols and gestures over the centuries, and the concentration of liturgical perspective toward the eternal converged in such a way that a "mighty" liturgical style emerged and is now fixed.[4]

Indeed, the Council Fathers at Vatican II seem to confirm Guardini's observation when they insist that liturgical rites ought to radiate a *noble simplicity* (*Sacrosanctum concilium*, 34: "*Ritus nobili simplicitate fulgeant*"). The *Novus ordo* does not eradicate this style. Far from it: the sharpening of the rites and the elimination of certain repetitions configure the liturgy more and more to the stateliness of the Greek temple and the elegant quiet of a Giotto painting.

Details, Details, Details ...

This grand style is manifest in the words, gestures, colors, and music of the liturgy. Guardini has already demonstrated in chapter 1 of *The Spirit of the Liturgy* that the language of liturgical prayer leads by thought, and not by emotion. Here he points out that the stylized form of the Roman collect is emphatically more distilled and universal than the language used in private prayer to God.

---

[4] Ibid., 309.

Liturgical language will be more remote from a pedestrian, personal, or particularly local use of language. Whatever one may think of the revised translations in the Third *Editio Typica* of the Roman Missal, the language resonates with what Guardini articulates about the liturgy's style. Liturgical dress, liturgical vessels, and even liturgical colors have also gone through a process whereby the particular and historical have been transfigured—"intensified" and "tranquilized"—in order to reach this note of universal currency.[5]

Let us consider, for instance, the Eucharistic host. It no longer directly resembles a morsel torn from a loaf of bread; rather, the bread-morsel has been simplified, intensified, flattened-out like the surface of a Giotto painting. The liturgical host is bread divested of any local peculiarity of mixing, forming, and firing ground wheat and water. And yet the host *is* bread, liturgically stylized for the Holy Sacrifice of the Mass, a ritual that itself ruptures the division between time and eternity, between earth and heaven. The host is that meeting place between the raw wheat of the high plains and the heavenly food of angels.

In terms of liturgical music, it is not the popular hymn but rather Gregorian chant that Guardini identifies as representative of this narrow sense of style. Fifteen years before *The Spirit of Liturgy*, Pius X's motu proprio *Tra le sollecitudini* had reasserted the use

[5] Ibid., 308.

of Gregorian chant in the liturgy, claiming that it is fittingly holy (not profane), representative of true art, and *universal* in nature (2–3).[6]

Guardini assists us further in envisioning how and why this music is most suited to the liturgy's style. Gregorian chant simplifies the singularity and complexity of other musical modalities; it distills sound and expression, refusing to call attention to itself. Its spare atmosphere and purified sound welcomes universal participation.

Modern Baggage

If the Catholic liturgy is to be the supreme and objective rule of the spiritual life κατὰ τὸν ὅλον (for all times and cultures)—as Guardini boldly announces at the opening of his liturgical classic—a liturgy falling short of the style he depicts would fail in some measure to achieve this universality and objectivity. This is a potent mandate for attending with care to the appearance of every official public worship of the Church. Do the People of God desire this universal style sufficiently enough?

Guardini anticipated objections to this liturgical style, objections that will no doubt sound familiar to our ears a hundred years later. "Modern" individuals,

---

[6] Pius XII's 1947 Encyclical *Mediator Dei* (192) and the Second Vatican Council's *Sacrosanctum concilium* (116) would also reiterate a preference for Gregorian chant in the liturgy.

he writes, would prefer a style that more directly addresses their own inner life. Would not that large group of American Catholics who today forgo the liturgy because they "get nothing out of it", because they can find nothing in the liturgy's cold and restrictive style that "speaks" to them, confess openly this "modern" predilection?

The careful arrangement of the parts of the liturgy, its generalized thought, and its formality of gesture have no immediate appeal and can often chafe against the individual's interior disposition and emotional impulses.[7] To be sure, some congregations would prefer to fill the empty foreground of the liturgy with cultural and self-referential additions, with words and prayers and music that make the spirit (and the ego) more vibrantly throb.

How does Guardini respond to this "modern" protest? On more than one occasion in the book, this perceived difficulty with the liturgy's style is resolved by an instruction about the value and place of private prayer and devotions. The arena for interpersonal warmth and emotive religious expression is located in the wide purview of pious devotions that legitimately and necessarily supplement the Church's official public prayer. In fact, Guardini acknowledges that the grand style of the liturgy could not be fully effective without the exercise and outlet of personal prayer and devotions.

[7] Guardini, *Spirit of the Liturgy*, 310.

With charm, he has called these extra-liturgical devotions "receptacles" into which believers can "pour their hearts".[8] So, gatherings of college youth, for example, during which "Praise and Worship" music pointedly enflames the emotions of believers, have their proper place and can be fruitful for a fuller participation in the solemn rites of the Mass or in the praying of the Liturgy of the Hours.

Creative Tension

Private prayer and devotion, measured by and oriented toward the Church's liturgy, ought also to excite desire for the rites of the Church. For Guardini, the evident polarity between the grand climate of the liturgy and the aegis of personal prayer ought to be construed, not as "mutually contradictory", but rather as mutually cooperative.[9] The tension is a creative and spiritually healthy one.

Guardini teaches us that a heuristic guidance should be offered to those who expect that the liturgy should carry the same personal and emotional valence as private devotions. Is the worshipper therefore mistaken who arrives at Sunday Mass expecting a warm and personal encounter with the Jesus who walked the streets

[8] Ibid., 290n9.
[9] Ibid., 313.

of Nazareth, hugged his mother, Mary, and laughed and cried with his disciples? In a word, yes.

Guardini acknowledges (and this in 1918—before the phenomena of mega-churches!) that Protestant-ism has "sometimes" faulted Catholic liturgy for providing only a "cold" and intellectualist concept of Jesus (Giotto's Jesus, for instance) rather than conveying the living man (the Grünewald Jesus). To be sure, the modern believer might yearn to encounter a warm intimacy with the man Jesus; yet, the Jesus who appears in the Catholic liturgy is the High Priest who sits at the right hand of the Father, the great Mediator between man and God, the one who shall return as Judge at the end of time, and the one who is Head of his Body the Church.[10] Indeed, though the glorified God-Man descends to feed us with himself at the Eucharistic altar, he does so to make us ever more like himself and to prepare us for eternal life around the heavenly altar.

Style Points

To my mind, Guardini's underscoring that "some-thing of us belongs to eternity" and that the style of the liturgy recalls us to this truth is perhaps the most requisite point of this chapter. Guardini wishes

[10] Ibid., 311.

us to see that only a truly authentic "Catholic style" of liturgy—"*actual* and universally comprehensible"—is capable of orienting and summoning the human soul to that full and desired knowledge of, and union with, the Creator. The simplifying, universalizing, and "tranquilizing" (what a marvelous word!) style of the liturgy allows the soul to move about in a more "spacious" spiritual world, moving it to a recollection, as Augustine would have it, of supreme happiness, consummate joy.[11]

The grand and noble style of the liturgy temporarily removes the shackles of time. It works a release from the prison of the self and permits an experience of the eternal, of stillness, and of silence. The grand style of the liturgy, like the Giotto painting, promotes contemplation. We need frankly to ask, however, whether this majestic style of liturgy proves to be what the ordinary Catholic in North America experiences? This is not widely the case, I suspect. Far too frequently, this noble style has been corrupted by a foreground of busyness; its distinct order has been muddied by the filling up of its clean spaces—with yet another song, yet another announcement, yet another prayer for vocations, etc.

The silent interstices of the liturgy have all but vanished, replaced by hurried movement and tangible distaste for decorum and "empty" quietness. When

[11] Ibid., 315.

the liturgy becomes more a celebration of the local community—its expressive needs—then particularity and the present crowd the liturgy's still frame and its universal style recedes.

Liturgical Trunk Show?

Have our liturgies come to resemble that car trunk with suitcases and bags thrown in whichever way? Have we—not with malice, of course—profaned the style of the Church's public prayer by attempting to make it more into the image of our finite, anxiety-laden, control-seeking existence? Guardini's deeply pastoral sensibility envisioned that the spacious and distilled atmosphere of the Church's liturgy could restore the souls of his fellow Europeans. The style of the liturgy was, he thought, a vigorous counterpoint to the aggressive nationalistic fervor in fashion at the time of his writing. As chaplain to the youth movement Quickborn in the years after the war, Guardini placed the Catholic liturgy at the heart of this movement. In 1922, he received permission to employ the *missa recitata* (the "dialogue mass"), which allowed the people to enter the grand style of the liturgy more fully by reciting the responses of the altar servers and the ordinary of the Mass.

This visionary priest profoundly understood that the mighty style of the liturgy could reveal truth as a living reality, a reality to be contemplated by worshippers. In this second decade of the twenty-first century, Guardini challenges Catholics, clergy and laity alike, to let the grand and noble style of the liturgy have its way. Such a style ennobles the soul, inviting and permitting it to pass over into a realm of sacred openness. There, unencumbered by the self, the soul may see once more the stars, the heavens, the angels, and recall its eternal *patria*.

Chapter IV

The Symbolism of the Liturgy

Together Again for the First Time Everywhere

David W. Fagerberg

The mark of a profound thinker is sometimes saluted by talking about a "balance" that he is able to maintain. This is not meant as an accusation of relativism; it is instead meant as an appreciation of paradox. One perspective is placed in one tray of the scale, another is placed in the other tray, and the thinker maintains a balance between the truth of one and the truth of the other. However, while Romano Guardini maintained this same sort of method in whatever he studied, this description of the approach fails to do justice to Guardini's thought for two reasons.

Centrist Thinking

The first reason is that Guardini usually deals with more than two truths at a time. He feels more like a juggler finding the center point of a spinning plate than someone balancing two sides of a teeter-totter. He is standing on a wobble board and trying not to tip his balance toward any single point on the compass. In the center hub of the wheel is the Mass, and spokes leading in from the rim represent extreme positions he wants to moderate. If one looks at his whole book, one can find the following sets of pairs: grave–playful, socialist–individualist, will–knowledge, logos–ethos, universal style–idiosyncratic style, morally earnest–aesthetically pleased, public ritual–private piety. (I have probably missed some.)

In order to participate in the Mass, persons will have to come toward the center from their extremes, and although all persons are approaching the hub, they are each approaching it from a different direction. This makes the cost of appreciating the Mass unique to every person. For example, the grave person must come to appreciate the playfulness of the liturgy, while the aesthete must come from the other direction to appreciate the seriousness of the liturgy; the predominantly individualistic person must engage the fellowship of the liturgy, and the predominantly communalistic person must discover his individual responsibility in the liturgy; the person to whom will is most important must appreciate the liturgy's truth-displaying quality, and the person to whom knowledge is most important must come to value the willful commitment required. And so forth.

Furthermore, in order to be appreciated, the Mass exacts a toll that is different for each person, depending on his starting point. What it costs one to participate in the liturgy will be a different fee from—and perhaps opposite to—what another person will have to pay. Therefore, humility is required of all if they are going to move down the spoke from their position on the outer rim to the center of the liturgy.

In the fourth chapter of *The Spirit of the Liturgy*, Guardini presents another pair of truths for us to stabilize. It concerns the relationship between body and soul. There are people, on the one hand, who see body and soul as sharply defined and distinguished. There are people, on the other hand, who see body and soul as amalgamated and inextricably jumbled together. This pair is one of the many sets of opposing viewpoints that Guardini has identified. For the sake of easy reference ahead, let us refer to the former type of person as a "Divider" and the latter type as a "Blender".

Integral Integrity

But as we consult our compass to stabilize our thinking, there is a second way in which Guardini's thought is different from that of those who seek to attain a simple balance. In a balance, the two truths are left at opposite poles, and they do not touch each other. Tension between them is lessened by taking turns, perhaps, but the balance on a seesaw, for instance, means that each end cancels the other out: the weight on one end prevents the other end from sinking too low, and vice-versa. But Guardini instead proposes that in this pair—our Divider and Blender fellows— the ends of the poles need to be *integrated*, not just balanced; integrated, not just alternately considered as a matter of "fair play". Guardini seeks cooperation between the Divider and the Blender when it comes to the creation of symbols. Not willing to leave them in seclusion, not willing to alternate between them, not willing to simply balance them, he wants to integrate them. He wants more than a cease-fire; he wants col- laboration between Divider and Blender. He wants them to be a team.

In this effort to get the two to play nice with each other, Guardini is not speaking about symbols them- selves but about approaches to symbols. He is speaking about two different personality types or perspectives. Yet the fact of these two different approaches leads to some central questions about symbolism in the liturgy, questions with which Guardini begins as he sketches the landscape. If God is above space, then what has he to do with directions as to specific localities? If God is above time, then what does time matter to him? If God is Simplicity, then how is he concerned with specific ritual, actions, and instruments? If God is a Spirit, then can matter have any significance in the soul's intercourse with him?

To sum up, Guardini is asking what the significance of liturgical symbolism is for the soul's intercourse with God, and to find an answer we must admit it depends on how the ego experiences the relationship between body and soul. Guardini is enough of a philosopher to know that the alternatives of dividing or blending the soul and body have been attempted at various times in the history of intellectual ideas. Cartesian rationalism created a centrifugal effect that moved mind and body apart; Germanic romanticism created a centripetal effect that moved mind and body together. The pendulum will continue to swing, Guardini knew, unless we can make peace between the approaches.

Approaching Truth

Here is how Guardini describes the Dividers. The spiritual plane appears entirely self-contained and lies beyond the physical plane. It has its existence, its reason, its purpose, its rationality, and does not really need the physical. The spiritual and physical are distinct orders, even if closely adjacent. When there is communication between them, as there must be, it is understood by this type of person to involve a transposition from the one plane into the other. Guardini sees this expressed in Leibniz's theory of monads, a theory of the universe that only contains God plus soul-like entities called monads, changing space and time and material objects into illusions.

For people who think this way, the physical has little to no importance; in fact, it appears to encumber and degrade spiritual activity. The soul cannot completely do away with the physical, but as far as the life of the soul is concerned, the physical is a burden. Is there any value to the physical for such people? Not much. It is an alloy, an aid to the elucidation of the spiritual, an illustration, an allegory. But the use of symbol is an imperfect concession in the spiritual and liturgical life. What the soul would rather do is attain its goals by purely spiritual means. The soul might have to use physical symbols, but it would rather not. Truth, moral impulse, beauty, knowledge, and practice of the good actually occur on a spiritual plane.

Here is how Guardini describes the Blenders. They see body and soul inextricably jumbled together and are inclined to amalgamate the two. Unification of soul and body is both possible and expected. The soul is a lining of the body; the body is the outside of the spirit. The body is visible soul. Belonging here are philosophical schools that speak of body as a condensation of soul or a materialization of spirit. Therefore, an external material action (in the human case, the action of the external body) is a manifestation of what the spirit is doing. If we like, we could make grander metaphysical claims and capitalize the word "spirit": the material and historical world is a manifestation of what the Spirit is doing. The Spirit, or men's spirits, enter into expression through nature, social forms, habits, clothing, substances.

Guardini's Move

If we left the descriptions of the two types of persons at that and placed them each on their own side of the balancing scale, Guardini admits we might be tempted to think that the Blender corresponds more closely to the nature of the liturgy, since it approves of the use of external phenomena to express an inner life. Liturgy uses action and material to express its spiritual verities—and a lesser thinker would leave it at that. A lesser thinker also would weigh in on the debate and defend either dividing or blending as a philosophical principle or an anthropological preference. But Guardini is a greater thinker, so he makes two moves.

First, he acknowledges that *both* personality types have a weakness. On the one hand, the Dividers fail to realize how vital the relationship is between the spiritual and the physical planes. They delimit boundaries, thus isolating and highlighting the spiritual plane, which is helpful in one way, but they do so with such vigor that all cohesion between the planes is lost. Because they prefer one over the other, they find liturgy challenging. On the other hand, the Blenders have the sense of cohesion missing in the Divider, but they lack objectiveness. Because they find it hard to adhere to defined formulas, defined actions, defined instruments, they also find liturgy challenging. For them, the symbol is an expression of the individual soul, but that individual soul is in a state of perpetual flux, and therefore the exterior expression (the symbol) is always in flux and in need of constantly new, fresh interpretation. Or change. Guardini says the Blender lacks one of the ingredients essential to the creation of symbols, but the Divider does not succeed any better.

Hence the second move Guardini makes. Having described the forte of each type of ego, and having noted the weakness each type of ego suffers, he attempts to make peace between them and integrate them. This attempt brings him to the concept of symbol, which "penetrates deeply into the essence and nature of the liturgy. What meaning has matter—regarded as the medium of spiritual receptivity and utterance, of spiritual impression and expression—for us?"[1]

In *Meditations before Mass*, Guardini affirms that "in the Liturgy everything is symbolic. But symbol is more than a corporal form representing something incorporeal."[2] In such a case, the exterior

[1] Romano Guardini, *The Spirit of the Liturgy*, trans. Ada Lane (1998), in Joseph Cardinal Ratzinger, *The Spirit of the Liturgy*, with Romano Guardini, *The Spirit of the Liturgy*, Commemorative edition (San Francisco: Ignatius Press, 2018), 316–17.

[2] Romano Guardini, *Meditations before Mass* (Manchester, N.H.: Sophia Institute Press, 2013), 40.

thing becomes no more than an allegory for spiritual truths. Guardini uses the example of the statue of the blindfolded woman holding scales as a representation of Justice. The person who sees this must be instructed as to the meaning of the bandaged eyes (no respecter of persons) and scales (measuring out equally). In an allegory, the meaning is not directly evident; it must be explained. "The Liturgy also contains allegories, but its basic forms are symbols. Their meaning is actually hidden, yet it reveals itself in a particular thing or person, much as the human soul, itself invisible, becomes perceptible, approachable in the expression and movements of a face. So it is in the church."[3]

Embodiment Ensouled

In Guardini's little book *Sacred Signs*, he reveals his own understanding of how body and soul relate. The liturgy, he claims, is not a matter of ideas; it is a matter of actual things, and things as they are now. "It is a continuous movement carried on by and through us, and its forms and actions issue from our human nature. To show how it arose and developed brings us no nearer to it.... What does help is to discern in the living liturgy what underlies the visible sign,

[3] Ibid.

to discover the soul from the body, the hidden and spiritual from the external and material. The liturgy has taken its outward shape from a divine and hidden series of happenings. It is sacramental in its nature."[4] In other words, the symbol in the liturgy is sacramental in its nature. Therefore, the liturgical symbols are elementary signs to which human nature responds, and Guardini indicates this process in the particular signs he discusses in *Sacred Signs*: signing oneself with the cross, hands, kneeling, standing, walking, striking the breast, steps, doors, candles, holy water, fire, ashes, incense, light and heat, bread and wine, linen, the altar, the chalice, the paten, blessing, space sanctified, bells, time sanctified, and the name of God. These signs are real symbols because they are things of the spirit fashioned into visible forms.

Matter has meaning for us when it becomes symbol. Matter can be the medium of spiritual receptivity when it becomes symbol. So in chapter 4 of *The Spirit of the Liturgy*, Guardini proposes that "a symbol may be said to originate when that which is interior and spiritual finds expression in that which is exterior and material."[5] By this he does not mean a general consent made by people, a common agreement to connect x with y. That would be allegory. The spiritual element is not coupled

---

[4] Romano Guardini, *Sacred Signs*, trans. Grace Branham (St. Louis: Pio Decimo Press, 1956), 9 (http://www.ewtn.com/catholicism/library/sacred-signs-11190).

[5] Guardini, *Spirit of the Liturgy*, 320.

with a material substance because we agree it should be so. "Rather must the spiritual element transpose itself into material terms because it is vital and essential that it should do so."[6] The Divider does not find it vital and essential that it do so; the Blender finds the spiritual element gets lost because the symbol proper is not circumscribed.

To make the point, we might borrow pairs of names for these personality types from a couple of other authors. In *Rite and Man*, Louis Bouyer contrasts different approaches to the liturgy by employing the opposing Christological heresies of Monophysitism and Nestorianism. To the former, "all ecclesiastical institutions, and especially the liturgy, seem to be equally sacred, and therefore immutable;"[7] the latter has "the tendency to stress the human aspects of Christianity in such a way that its individuality, along with its divinity, is in danger of disappearing".[8] Like the Blender, the Monophysite liturgist desires to keep things mysterious, hieratic, sacred (and, Bouyer admits, attributes this possibility to the exclusive use of Latin). Mystery means the unintelligible. Like the Divider, the Nestorian liturgist would discard symbols that have accrued across the history of the liturgy, returning to the primitive Supper, a meal in

[6] Ibid., 321.
[7] Louis Bouyer, *Rite and Man* (Notre Dame: University of Notre Dame Press, 1963), 5.
[8] Ibid., 7.

common among friends. Mystery means the hidden thing made intelligible.

Bouyer summarizes: "According to the Monophysite concept of Christianity, the Mass can only be the Mass by being something entirely different from ordinary life and completely separate from it.... According to the Nestorian concept, however, everything about the Mass should recall a profane meal, even to the inclusion of mundane conversations."[9] The Blender is so charmed by the symbolism of the altar that he forgets the table; the Divider has extracted the primitive table from out of the religious and Christian symbolism of altars to treat it alone.

Extremely Meaningful

In *Elements of Rite*, Aidan Kavanagh offers another contrasting pair of terms that might describe the two personality types. "Minimalism and pontificalism represent the two unacceptable extremes in degree of liturgical usage. The first sins by symbolic and ceremonial defect, the second by symbolic and ceremonial excess.... Pontificalism is always swollen, overblown, and fussy; minimalism is always shrunken, desiccated, and perfunctory."[10] A Blender is more enamored with the

---

[9] Ibid., 9.

[10] Aidan Kavanagh, *Elements of Rite* (New York: Pueblo Publishing, 1982). All the quotes in this paragraph come from pages 80–81.

symbol than with the reality it is carrying (preferring the box car to the freight), the way a pontificalist places "too much emphasis on tertiary elements to the point of obscuring the primary". A Divider thinks one only needs to do as much froufrou as is required to get the point across, the way a minimalist's service is "always insubstantial, placing not enough emphasis on anything". So Kavanagh concludes that "it is pontificalism which breeds the rumor that solemnity is synonymous with complexity, heavy-handedness, and boredom in the assembly; minimalism which breeds the rumor that being solemn about solemn things is a vice." The Blender wants *affective* symbol; the Divider is not sure how to make liturgy *effective*.

If we select any symbolic action in the liturgy, we can imagine it being done in one extreme or the other. Speech can be purple prose or a beige mumble; the architecture overly embellished or second-rate; the art flamboyant or insipid; the procession a strutting or a casual shuffle. These extremes explain one of the more cryptic remarks Guardini makes about walking in his famous 1964 letter to the Mainz liturgical conference:

> But those whose task it is to teach and educate will have to ask themselves—and this is all-decisive—whether they themselves desire that liturgical act or, to put it plainly, whether they know of its existence and what exactly it consists of and that it is neither

a luxury nor an oddity, but a matter of fundamental importance. Or does it, basically, mean the same to them as to the parish priest of the late nineteenth century who said: "We must organize the procession better; we must see to it that the praying and singing is done better". He did not realize that he should have asked himself quite a different question: how can the act of walking become a religious act, a retinue for the Lord progressing through his land, so that an 'epiphany' may take place.[11]

Guardini, in considering walking as a liturgical act, seeks a better understanding of liturgical renewal than merely shuffling the altar furniture, updating the rubrics, inserting teaching moments in the celebration, improving prayer and song, or better staging the procession. Liturgical renewal comes about when our actions—such as walking—become symbolic. And the way to appreciate symbol is to understand the body as natural emblem of the soul. The body-act of walking is a spiritual-act transposed onto the material plane. It is so transposed because it is vital and essential to do so. "The altar is not an allegory, but a symbol. The thoughtful believer does not have to be taught that it is a border, that 'above it' stretch inaccessible heights and 'beyond it' the reaches of divine remoteness; somehow he is aware of

---

[11] Unable to attend the third German Liturgical Congress, Guardini sent a letter to Msgr. Wagner, organizer of the conference, in 1964. See Romano Guardini, "The 'Liturgical Act' Today", *Antiphon* 5, no. 3 (2000).

this."[12] Somehow the thoughtful believer is aware of this if liturgy uses genuine symbols that suffer neither excess nor defect.

Universe of Symbols

A genuine symbol is occasioned by the spontaneous expression of an actual spiritual condition. Then a good symbol will rise above the purely individual plane and enjoy widespread currency. It will be universally comprehensible and significant. And here one must read chapters 3 and 4 in tandem. Guardini describes the universal currency expected of liturgy in the third chapter, and he is applying the thought in the fourth to the idea of symbol.

The Lord's Supper did not continue as a Passion Play; it was transformed into a universal currency that could be used in every culture and every century. Something of us belongs to eternity, and in order to "rise to the sphere which transcends the individual order and is therefore accessible to people of every condition, time, and place", the liturgy has style.[13] And formal style (i.e., arranged symbolism) makes possible the corporate dimension of the Church. In *The Church and the Catholic*, Guardini proposes a problem we might have with this understanding of

[12] Guardini, *Meditations before Mass*, 43.
[13] Guardini, *Spirit of the Liturgy*, 314.

formal style and lays it at the feet of modern individualism. "With the development of individualism since the end of the Middle Ages, the Church has been thought of as ... a viaduct of life but not as life itself. It has, in other words, been thought of as a thing exterior from which men might receive life, not a thing into which men must be incorporated that they may live with its life."[14]

As a result of this individualism, religion came to be considered something that belonged to the subjective sphere, and objective religion (as represented by the Church) was primarily the regulation of this individual and subjective religion. Thus, man "lived in a world of abstract forms and symbols, which was not linked up with the reality to which the symbols referred".[15] But that means the symbol never rises above the idiosyncratic, and the liturgy-as-symbol never becomes catholic and traditional. One cannot understand Guardini on liturgy without treating Guardini on ecclesiology.

Collaborative Liturgy

Therefore, Guardini concludes that both ego types—Dividers and Blenders—must cooperate in the creation of symbols. "The former type, then, must abandon

---

[14] Guardini, *The Church and the Catholic* (London: Aeterna Press, 2015), 1.
[15] Ibid., 2–3.

their exaggerated spirituality, admit the existence of the relationship between the spiritual and the physical, and freely avail themselves of the wealth of liturgical symbolism.... The latter type must endeavor to stem their extravagance of sensation, and to bind the vague and ephemeral elements into clear-cut forms."[16] Then the liturgical symbol becomes a universal possession by exceeding the solitary, historical incident that occasioned it. The Last Supper can symbolically extend its substantial reality to us, although we live centuries later and in a different culture. The Mass is symbol, not allegory, not historical reproduction, not representation. In showing us this truth, Guardini does not tip the scales one way or another for our Blender or our Divider; rather, he recalibrates the scale in a way that invites both sides to weigh their own strengths and weaknesses against the greater reality of the liturgy itself.

[16] Guardini, *Spirit of the Liturgy*, 323–24.

Chapter V

The Playfulness of the Liturgy

At Prayer in the Fields of the Lord

Father Daniel Cardó

It is ironic that the serious question about the apparent "uselessness" of the liturgy is answered by invoking the playfulness in the liturgy. This is the genius of the fifth chapter of Romano Guardini's *The Spirit of the Liturgy*.

Guardini's reflections on the playfulness of the liturgy have been influential in different areas of thought. Johan Huizinga quoted chapter 5 in his classic *Homo Ludens* (1938) on play as a decisive element in culture.[1] Josef Pieper, a student of Guardini, echoes his master in his philosophical reflections on *Leisure: the Basis of Culture* (1952), where he shows the centrality

---

[1] See Johan Huizinga, Homo Ludens: *A Study of the Play-Element in Culture* (Boston: Beacon Press, 1967), 19.

of leisure for culture, with worship at its core.[2] And Joseph Ratzinger in his main work on liturgy (*The Spirit of the Liturgy*, 2000) honors Guardini's short but influential volume. The future Benedict XVI begins his work with an explicit reference to the idea of the liturgy as play, highlighting the richness but also the limits of this image.[3]

Put in Play

Why is the liturgy compared to play? What can we learn today from this idea? Let us first understand what Guardini said about this relationship between play and liturgy and then reflect on the importance of this contribution for us today, a hundred years after these words were written.

So let us begin again by asking a more primary set of questions: Why is the liturgy so full of complicated rituals and elaborate prayers? What is the actual need, at Mass, for all the exact instructions for the ceremonies that surround what, seemingly, would be a rather simple action: the Eucharistic Consecration?

Guardini's main answer requires the careful distinction between purpose and meaning. Purpose is an

---

[2] See Josef Pieper, *Leisure: The Basis of Culture* (San Francisco: Ignatius Press, 2009), 15.

[3] Joseph Cardinal Ratzinger, *The Spirit of the Liturgy*, trans. John Saward (2000), in Ratzinger, *Spirit of the Liturgy*, with Guardini, *Spirit of the Liturgy*, Commemorative edition (San Francisco: Ignatius Press, 2018), 27–28.

organizing principle that subordinates actions toward an external goal. Projects and professions are normally organized by their purpose. But there are things in life that are purpose-*less*. Nature is a clear example: What is the actual practical need for so many shapes, colors, scents, and flavors? These are things that are "purpose-less, but still full of meaning;"[4] aimless, but significant. Along with nature, we can think of the life of the soul, philosophical knowledge, and art: while these realities have no practical finality, they are full of meaning. They can be judged, not on the criterion of functionality, but on that of significance, of meaningful existence.

These two principles—purpose and meaning—should not be seen as opposed to each other. The life of the Church shows their coexistence. As there are practical needs of administration and organization, the Church has a system of laws and ecclesiastical government that is an important part of her life. But, of course, there is in the Church "another side": that which is free of functional practicality and has no need for an external goal to justify its existence. The liturgy is not a means to attain a certain practical objective but is an end in itself: the act of glorifying and contemplating God's majesty.

This truth is apparent to anyone who pays attention to the abundance of liturgical prayers and rituals. Although there is certain organization based on seasons and feasts, no detailed plan of instruction or clear

---

[4] Romano Guardini, *The Spirit of the Liturgy*, trans. Ada Lane (1998), in Ratzinger, *Spirit of the Liturgy*, 328.

and distinct purpose can be found in the liturgical life of the Church. Is this a waste of time? Do we find here a missed opportunity?

Guardini reflects at this point on two scriptural passages. The first one is Ezekiel's vision of the Cherubim moved by the Spirit in contemplation of God's glory (chapter 10). The second one is Proverbs 8:30–31: "I was beside him, like a master workman; and I was daily his delight, rejoicing before him always, rejoicing in his inhabited world." The Son "rejoices" before the Father, full of meaning, playfulness, and pure happiness, with a delight that goes beyond any practical purpose.

In our earthly life, there are two realities that offer an image of this "sublime uselessness": the play of the child and the creation of the artist. Children do not aim at a specific functional objective when they play: they pour themselves forth in countless movements and words that beautifully express the richness of life. Artists try to give life to their being and longings without a necessary didactic aim.

The sacred liturgy, while being similar to these realities, offers something even greater: the possibility of becoming, with the aid of divine grace, a child of God. And, as this demands going beyond ordinary experience, the liturgy finds its expressions in the world of art. Thus, liturgy "unites art and reality in a supernatural childhood before God".[5] And there is

[5] Ibid., 335.

nothing more important than this purposeless action. We see a glimpse of this gravity in the earnestness that children have in setting up the rules for their games and that artists have in their pursuit of the right form.

This is what the liturgy does: with "endless care", it has "laid down the serious rules of the sacred game that the soul plays before God".[6] The greatness of the liturgy consists not only in producing wonderful works of art, but in transforming us "into living works of art before God",[7] becoming thus as little children. This is God's solemn and joyful invitation: to "live liturgically", to be children of the Father, to be not afraid of "wasting time", of "playing", of "celebrating", of "existing" in the peaceful presence of the Eternal Father.

Paradoxically, it is here, says Guardini, that an essential didactic aim ought to be found in the liturgy: to learn the simplicity of prayer and abandonment, renouncing the oppression of always asking "why?" and "what for?"—of seeking a functional purpose to all that we do. Only in this way will we be able "to play the divinely ordained game of the liturgy in liberty and beauty and holy joy before God".[8] This is, truly, an anticipation of eternal life, which far from being some boring, endless, and fruitless passivity, will be the consummation of our existence in an unending song of praise.

[6] Ibid., 336.
[7] Ibid., 337.
[8] Ibid.

Play Today

Guardini's reflections on the playfulness of the liturgy
are beautiful. The reader is at times struck by the musi-
cality and poetic tone of some paragraphs, which are
perceived even more keenly against the background
of a book that, generally speaking, is very precise yet
theoretical. It only makes sense: the sublime purposelessness of the liturgy is, indeed, a beautiful gift that
the act of glorifying God pours into the human heart.

Needless to say, the analogy of the liturgy as play
cannot be perfect. Ratzinger, in his own *The Spirit of the
Liturgy*, pointed out two of its limitations. First, he says,
since the rules of certain games or sports can become
burdensome, it is essential to indicate *what* we are playing. The second limitation of this comparison is that the
idea of the life to come remains only too vague.[9]

Aware of its merits and limitations, let us reflect
now on some ways in which the idea of the "playfulness of the liturgy" can make a relevant contribution
to the liturgical life of the Church today, particularly
with regard to active participation.

Roles and Rules

One of the most important concepts that the Church
has repeated since the dawn of the twentieth century

---

[9] See Ratzinger, *Spirit of the Liturgy*, 28–29.

is that of *actuosa participatio*. It is a reference, not merely or mainly to external activity, but to an interior movement: rather than being passive spectators, all the faithful are called actually to take part in what is celebrated in the liturgical act.

The oversimplification of active participation as doing things and multiplying visible roles for as many people as possible during the liturgy has been a serious source of confusion. The analogy of play can prove helpful here.

Everyone knows that in any good game there are roles and rules. If all the participants were to claim the right to do what they pleased or invent roles in order to have a more active part, that game would certainly fail. If the game is to be good, there is a need for balance: knowing its rules and actually playing it.

Knowing every single rule of a game does not mean playing it well (or even enjoying the game very much, either). On the other hand, playing the game without knowing its logic and basic dynamic only leads to failure. We need both: rules and action. In this way we can enter into the free and different world of a game.

It is the same with the liturgy. To take part actually in its action, we need to know what happens in it and do our part. This demands a twofold act of trust in the game of the liturgy: trust in the rules (i.e., the rite) and trust in the players (i.e., the celebrant and the faithful).

In Rites We Trust

Extending the analogy of play, we could say that the rules of the game of the liturgy are found in its rite. The liturgical rite must be followed with reverence and appreciation for its value. For rather than being an arbitrary and ultimately disposable set of procedures, the rite is the path to the mystery, developed slowly and organically through the centuries. Indeed, as Benedict XVI wrote about Christ's command *do this* at the Last Supper, the Lord had the "expectation that the Church, born of his sacrifice, will receive this gift, developing under the guidance of the Holy Spirit the liturgical form of the sacrament".[10]

It is this form, with its specific words and actions, that needs to be known, esteemed, and respected. Doubtless, the wisdom of millennia, with the countless generations that have faithfully prayed according to the "rules" of the liturgy, bearing abundant fruits of holiness and charity, ought to be greater than anyone's individual creativity.

To promote a renewed appreciation of the liturgical rite, we need to grow in our comprehension of it. Two privileged paths for this task are the *ars celebrandi* and mystagogical formation.

---

[10] Benedict XVI, Post-Synodal Apostolic Exhortation *Sacramentum caritatis*, on the Eucharist as the Source and Summit of the Church's Life and Mission (February 22, 2007), 11.

According to Cardinal Ranjith, former secretary in the Congregation for Divine Worship and Discipline of the Sacraments, the priest's art of celebrating (*ars celebrandi*) is first and foremost the art of conforming oneself to Christ the High Priest.[11] This interior disposition becomes devout fidelity to the rite of the Church. In turn, a priest truly committed to the *ars celebrandi* will offer the serene and radiant experience of the mystery of the sacred liturgy without compromises or rationalizations. This experience will lead the people to see, hear, smell, taste, and touch the signs of salvation. There will be no need of useless explanations: only a "simple vision", in the words of Josef Pieper, "to which truth offers itself like a landscape to the eye".[12]

The main demand of this art will be to trust in the power of the symbolic ritual of the liturgy and appreciate anew the capacity of intuitive knowledge. In a practical way, the celebrant of the liturgy should not be afraid of a language that speaks of a different world: words that are beautiful and eloquent; gestures that are visible and powerful; vestments that show the beauty and dignity of the liturgical action; nobility in the sacred vessels and buildings; music that leads into the mystery of God and is not limited to the expression of our own spiritual experience. It is a

[11] See "Toward an Ars Celebrandi in Liturgy", *Adoremus*, March 15, 2009, https://www.adoremus.org/2009/03/15/Toward-an-Ars-Celebrandi-in -Liturgy/.

[12] Pieper, *Leisure: The Basis of Culture*, 28.

matter, not of blindly following rubrics, but rather of entering into the mystery.

More concretely: a blessing should be clearly seen by everyone as the expressive gesture of the cross, sealed by a noble movement of the arm. The anointing with the sacred chrism at Baptism or Confirmation should be so generous that the symbolic aroma of the consecrated oil can be perceived as a sign of Christ's sweet aroma. The elevation of the consecrated Host and chalice should be done without haste, accompanied by the reverence proper to such a holy moment, enhanced with the sounds of bells, and, especially on solemnities, enshrined by the light shed by candles and the smoke expressed by incense. In this way, priests will offer an ample entry into the mystery of the liturgy.

The intuitively perceived *ars celebrandi* should be accompanied by a mystagogical path of formation. Our catechetical programs should include more mystagogy, in order to lead those being formed in the faith, particularly those preparing to receive a sacrament, into the mysteries where they will receive the life of grace. Our homilies could also be enriched by frequent mystagogical reflections. Not only are these very attractive to our people, but they also offer abundant material for an ongoing education in what we all do in our liturgical celebrations. The Fathers of the Church are a shining and imitable example of this kind of preaching. In their words we find the fine art of preparing the hearts of believers for the liturgical events of salvation without an excessive rationalistic explanation, leaving room for the mystery to speak loudly for itself, just as in the fine image provided by William Harmless:[13] a movie critic will create expectation, telling us what a movie is about without spoiling the experience of watching it directly. This kind of formation and preaching is only possible when there is an honest trust in the power of the rite (the "rules of the game") and in the capacity of the faithful (the "players") to receive and comprehend what God achieves through the liturgy. This leads us to our next point.

Playing Human

Guardini famously asked in a letter to the 1964 Liturgical Conference in Mainz, in the face of the challenges of modernity for liturgical reform: "Would it not be better to admit that man in this industrial and scientific age, with its new sociological structure, is no longer capable of a liturgical act?"[14]

It would seem that many liturgists would immediately respond in the affirmative to this question: an average person of our times is not really capable of a

---

[13] See William Harmless, *Augustine and the Catechumenate* (Collegeville, Minn.: Liturgical Press, 2014), 422.

[14] Romano Guardini, "The 'Liturgical Act' Today", *Antiphon* 5, no. 3 (2000): 48.

liturgical act. Consequently, because of this lack of trust in the "liturgical capacity" of the modern or postmodern person, the liturgy would need to be adapted and simplified; it should always be completely understandable to our reason, and it must not include elements that are not familiar from daily experience. Furthermore, some liturgists might argue, if we want to keep our people in the pews, we need to reduce the mystery and solemnity of the rite, introducing enjoyable surprises and a positive tone to what we do and say.

We all have heard wordy comments explaining rites and gestures that interrupt the flow of the ritual, assuming that without them we cannot grasp their meaning; we all have seen the arms of cantors raised high before congregations, as if we were incapable of realizing when to sing "Alleluia!" We all have heard homilies so full of stories and jokes, as if we were not capable of following a simple argument, and we all have experienced the shortest forms of rituals at the most important feasts, as if no one could enjoy the calm of a well-executed ceremony over an extended period of time. Are not the liturgical accommodations enumerated above (now hardened into common trends) rather condescending? Should we not trust more in the capacity of the human heart and offer in the liturgy what the heart is truly looking for? As Augustine said: "What does our soul desire more passionately than truth?"[15] The human

---

[15] Saint Augustine, *In Johannis Evangelium Tractatus,* tractate 26, para. 5 (PL 35:1609).

heart, even in a time of relativism and confusion such as ours, still desires the truth. And it is in the sacred liturgy, most especially in the Eucharist, that we can encounter the truth of life.[16]

This desire for truth appears to be particularly relevant for young people. While in no way being the only factor, the general oversimplification of liturgical celebrations in the past decades has not proven particularly fruitful for young people in the practice of their faith. According to a recent Public Religion Research Institute study, only 7 percent of young adults raised Catholic still attend Mass.[17]

Truth Is in Play

Much has been said about millennials. One thing is true: they reject what is fake; they like authenticity. They want good things; they care for complex flavors; they appreciate uncompromising beauty. Unsurprisingly, they like games: board games that are intricate and demand attention, discipline, rules, time, and ceremony. And, also unsurprisingly, they are drawn to beautiful liturgies that are celebrated with art and without compromise.

---

[16] See Benedict XVI, *Sacramentum caritatis*, 2.
[17] Betsy Cooper et al., "Exodus: Why Americans Are Leaving Religion— and Why They're Unlikely to Come Back", PRRI, September 22, 2016, https://www.prri.org/research/prri-rns-poll-nones-atheist-leaving-religion/.

Millennials like music that is well performed; they are attracted to chant and to hymns of beautiful melody and theology. They do not instinctively reject the use of Latin; they appreciate the symbolic power of incense. They are grateful for homilies that challenge them and elevate their horizons. They are fascinated by the mystery. For they can understand that the liturgy is a kind of sacred play, with beautiful rules and capable participants, who are grateful to find their joy as they kneel down to adore, as good children, their Father in heaven.

Chapter VI

The Seriousness of the Liturgy

Some Good and Weighty Truths about Beauty

Bishop James D. Conley

"The liturgy is art", wrote Romano Guardini one hundred years ago, "translated into terms of life".[1]

In the sacred liturgy, he said, "the Creator-Artist, the Holy Spirit, has garnered and expressed the whole fullness of reality and of creative art."[2] Understanding that liturgy expresses the fullness of reality, of truth itself, is critical to understanding the liturgy, to praying and offering it, and to being transformed by it.

The Church offers the liturgy, Guardini wrote, for the worship of God and because of our "desperate

---

[1] Romano Guardini, *The Spirit of the Liturgy*, trans. Ada Lane (1998), in Joseph Cardinal Ratzinger, *The Spirit of the Liturgy*, with Romano Guardini, *The Spirit of the Liturgy*, Commemorative edition (San Francisco: Ignatius Press, 2018), 338.

[2] Ibid., 339.

spiritual need. It is to give expression to the events of the Christian's inner life: the assimilation, through the Holy Spirit, of the life of the creature to the life of God in Christ; the actual and genuine rebirth of the creature into a new existence; the development and nourishment of this life, its stretching forth from God in the Blessed Sacrament and the means of grace toward God in prayer and sacrifice; and all this in the continual mystic renewal of Christ's life in the course of the ecclesiastical year."[3]

The sixth chapter of Guardini's masterwork, *The Spirit of the Liturgy*, argues that liturgy "undertakes the molding and adapting of human entities on behalf of the Kingdom of God", that "it is primarily concerned with reality, with the approach of a real creature to a real God, and with the profoundly real and serious matter of redemption."[4]

Get Serious Now

Guardini's vision of liturgy is serious. Liturgy is a serious work—a work of the Lord and a work of the Church—and to serve its sacred and noble purpose, it must be beautiful. Beauty, Guardini writes, "is the full, clear, and inevitable expression of the inner truth

[3] Ibid., 349.
[4] Ibid., 340, 349.

in the external manifestation ..., the splendid perfection that dwells in the revelation of essential truth
and goodness".[5]

Beauty in the liturgy reveals what is true and good,
makes it manifest, expressed, and perceived, not as
"mere lifeless accuracy of comprehension", but as
"the right and appropriate regulation of life, a vital
spiritual essence ..., the intrinsic value of existence in
all its force and fullness".[6]

Through beautiful liturgy, Guardini says, we
encounter "the triumphant splendor that breaks forth
when the hidden truth is revealed, when the external
phenomenon is at all points the perfect expression
of the inner essence".[7] Through beautiful liturgy,
we encounter the Lord, expressed and revealed in
his glory, and we are transformed by him. In the liturgy, he writes, the Church herself is "in the process
of transformation".[8]

Beauty stands in close relation to truth and goodness, while remaining an independent value, Guardini
writes. But there must be something behind beauty
in order for it to reveal itself externally. One could
say that beauty is truth and goodness made visible.
But in the end, it is truth that wins out. Guardini
writes that "pride of place, therefore, though not of

[5] Ibid., 342.
[6] Ibid., 343.
[7] Ibid.
[8] Ibid., 341.

rank or worth, belongs, not to beauty, but to truth".[9] He points out that the philosophers have always taught that beauty is the splendor of truth. In Guardini's words, "beauty is the triumphant splendor that breaks forth when the hidden truth is revealed, when the external phenomenon is at all points the perfect expression of the inner essence."[10]

For Guardini, the liturgy is to be beautiful in order to manifest its essential truth, and for the good of the salvation of souls, especially our own. The beauty of the liturgy offers us a palpable, sensible, real experience of the reality of the Incarnation, the Resurrection, and our own redemption.

Beauty in the liturgy matters. It is essential to our sacred worship. But there is a danger, Guardini says, "of beauty being placed before truth or treated as entirely separate from the latter".[11] Because the beauty of the liturgy is important, there is a danger that it might be considered apart from truth, Guardini warned, fostering an attitude that "ultimately degenerates into nerveless aestheticism".[12]

Such aestheticism has no place in the "Opus Dei" of Christian worship. Indeed, Guardini says, those who approach liturgy to worship, to seek strength and consolation, who experience transformation in Christ

---

[9] Ibid., 343.
[10] Ibid.
[11] Ibid., 344.
[12] Ibid.

through sacred worship, "penetrate far more deeply into the essence of the liturgy than does the connoisseur who is busy savoring the contrast between the austere beauty of a Preface and the melodiousness of a Gradual".[13]

Always Is Now

One hundred years after the publication of *The Spirit of the Liturgy*, the idea of many people savoring, or even recognizing, a preface or a gradual seems unlikely. Indeed, the ordinary experience of sacred worship for most Catholics has changed so dramatically since the time of Guardini's work that it seems to many that his reflections are irrelevant to the current state of sacred liturgy in the life of the Church.

But Guardini's work was prescient, and is relevant to our circumstances, because his reflections on beauty, truth, and sacred worship are perennial. And indeed, his thoughts, and his warnings, have a particular importance as we reflect on the development of sacred liturgy since the time of the reforms called for by *Sacrosanctum concilium*.

The Second Vatican Council's efforts for a reform of sacred liturgy were needed in large part in order to foster the kind of transformative experience in sacred

[13] Ibid., 339.

worship called for by Guardini and his collaborators in the liturgical movement. The "fully conscious, and active participation in liturgical celebrations"[14] desired by *Sacrosanctum concilium* was a call for all Catholics to understand the work of sacred liturgy, its meaning, and to offer their sacrifices in union with the sacrifice of Christ at Calvary and at the altar.

But the implementation of *Sacrosanctum concilium* and the celebration of the Mass of Paul VI have often left much to be desired. And in many cases, this is because of the kind of aestheticism about which Guardini warned.

The aesthetic preferences, of course, of many misguided efforts to implement the liturgical developments of the Second Vatican Council have not been those anticipated by Guardini. But the underlying concerns are the same. He was concerned with the effects of Protestant individualism, with emotivism, and, at the same time, with a certain kind of formalism that had diminished the capacity of the faithful to engage, consciously and actively, in the liturgical act of worship. The liturgical movement sought to rediscover the Church's sacred liturgical traditions, precisely in order to imbue in the Church a sense of what it meant to worship, in spirit and in truth, and to be transformed by the sacred liturgy.

---

[14] Vatican Council II, Constitution on the Sacred Liturgy *Sacrosanctum concilium* (December 4, 1963), 14.

Theater of the Absurd

Sacrosanctum concilium has often been misunderstood by those who have separated truth from aesthetics, who have responded to individualism with a kind of foppish pseudo-communalism, bereft of communion with the sacred Trinity, or who have confused the accidental changes to the liturgy with the essential purposes of the council and, thereby, misunderstood the relationship between essential beauty in the liturgy and transformation in Christian holiness.

Guardini made mention of aesthetes savoring the differences between graduals and prefaces. The aesthetes of the postconciliar era have been of a different sort. But nevertheless, their confusion has led to the kind of "spiritual theater"[15] about which Guardini warned.

Consider the kinds of aberrations and innovations that have sometimes plagued the sacred liturgy in the postconciliar period. Consider the ways they embody a preference for aesthetics over sacred worship—a limited kind of aesthetics, to be sure, but aesthetics nonetheless. Consider the music, art and architecture, or *modus celebrandi* that have been paeans of liturgical theater, expressions of the aesthetic preferences of the celebrant, the "worship director", or the liturgist, but not expressions of the ineffable truth of the sacred liturgy. Guardini's work was prescient

[15] Guardini, *Spirit of the Liturgy*, 350.

because it understood that the fleeting dictates of aestheticism are a temptation for anyone who strives to make a beautiful thing and forgets that it is the Lord who is the source of all that is true, who has given us the form of real beauty, and who wishes to inspire and transform us in and through true beauty.

The greatest victims of postconciliar aestheticism have been the ordinary Catholics, those about whom the liturgical movement was most concerned, who, as a consequence of shallow aestheticism, have often missed out on the meaning of the sacred mystery of the Mass, celebrated directly in front of them. From a desire to make the Mass more "accessible", it has often become more hidden, its mysteries shrouded in banality, rather than proclaimed and revealed in staggering and timeless beauty.

Mass Celebration

The Mass is the Mass, whether it is celebrated with great beauty or reverence or whether it is celebrated according to the whims of aestheticism and the tempting siren song of "liturgical theater". But absent the dazzling clarity of beauty, the meaning of the Mass, and its potential to transform us, is lost on those who are called to celebrate it or to assist in its celebration.

This is the reason why *Liturgiam authenticam* sought to preserve a certain kind of sacral beauty in the language of the liturgy—to reveal, for the good of the salvation of souls, the extraordinary sacral nature of the mystery of the Holy Sacrifice of the Mass.

Liturgy is "primarily concerned with reality, with the approach of a real creature to a real God, and with the profoundly real and serious matter of redemption", writes Guardini. "There is here no question of creating beauty, but only that of finding salvation for sin-stricken humanity. Here truth is at stake, and the fate of the soul, and real—yes, ultimately the only real—life. All this it is that must be revealed, expressed, sought after, found, and imparted by every possible means and method; and when this is accomplished, lo! it is turned into beauty."[16]

In All Seriousness

Why, then, does Guardini title the sixth chapter of his work "The Seriousness of Liturgy"? Worship is serious because sin is serious, and redemption is serious business. Liturgy must, by every means and method, draw up the faithful into the drama of the reality of our redemption, transforming each one of us in wonder for holy living in union with Almighty

[16] Ibid., 349.

God. Liturgy must be beautiful, in every possible way, because every glimmer of beauty might point some soul to the glimmering truth, goodness, and beauty of the Lord. In short, the liturgy is serious because these elements of the liturgy are as serious as sin.

Guardini understood this, and so did the Fathers of the Second Vatican Council. So did the great admirer of Guardini, Pope Emeritus Benedict XVI. His great work, *The Spirit of the Liturgy*, named as an homage to Guardini, intended to translate the ideas of Guardini to his own time. We must continue to translate those ideas—that sacred worship matters—because it is the sanctifying summit of the Christian life in our own time. And those who continue the reform and renewal of sacred liturgy in the life of the Church do just that.

To make beautiful liturgy, of course, requires an intimate knowledge of the serious truths that beauty reveals. Beautiful liturgy does not begin with the aesthetic preferences of the celebrant. It does not even begin with the treasures of the Church's liturgical tradition. Beautiful liturgy begins with real and intimate union with the Lord. To undertake the work of beautiful liturgy, which is really a work of the Holy Spirit, we must know and understand the promptings and movements of the Spirit, and we must know and understand the person of the Incarnate Word of God. Beautiful liturgy—serious liturgy, to be sure—depends entirely on intimate and authentic unity with the one whom we worship. Absent that, regardless of the accidents of music, word, and movement, we cannot worship the Lord beautifully or draw others into the serious beauty of the Trinity.

Pray One and All

One other point of Guardini's must remain clear. Beautiful liturgy is not for the elite, it is not to be "the delicate morsel for the connoisseur",[17] it is not to be celebrated only in enclaves of the like-minded. No, the entire Church needs the beauty of the liturgy. And so those who know the power and potential of beauty must be missionaries of beauty in every ordinary and common part of the Church's life. Every soul needs the grace of beautiful liturgy.

True beauty, Guardini wrote, is modest. And those who seek to reform the reform of the Church's life must be modest, too, patient, generous, and virtuous. "Liturgy must chiefly be regarded from the standpoint of salvation",[18] Guardini writes. For the sake of souls' salvation, we must continue to work with generosity and charity, for an "Opus Dei" of beauty in the work of sacred liturgy.

[17] Ibid., 348.
[18] Ibid., 350.

Chapter VII

The Primacy of the Logos over the Ethos

By Neither Word nor Bread Alone

Father Emery de Gaál

"In the beginning was the Word, and the Word was with God, and the Word was God.... And the Word became flesh and dwelt among us, full of grace and truth; we have beheld his glory, glory as of the only-begotten Son from the Father" (Jn 1:1,14). In the concluding chapter of *The Spirit of Liturgy*, Romano Guardini thrusts the reader into the dilemma of the highly learned scholar Faust in the quintessentially German play *Faust* by Johann Wolfgang von Goethe (1749–1832): Does the Word or the Deed enjoy pride of place? That is, which is more fundamental in the Christian life: knowledge and truth (*Logos*) or will and action (*Ethos*)? After pondering this question, Faust, in the manner of a usurper and revolutionary, "corrects" the prologue to John's Gospel and writes "not 'In the beginning was the Word', but 'In the beginning was the Deed.' "[1]

The Spirit of the Liturgy was first published in 1918, republished twenty-five times in German, and is now available in not less than ten languages. Today the book continues to challenge us to offer a Christian response to Faust.

To understand how the liturgy provides such a response, guiding the will according to truth, it is important to visit the Faustian tension to which Guardini draws our attention in this final chapter—"The Primacy of the Logos over the Ethos", that is, the Word over the Deed. In order to understand this distinction, in turn, we take a helpful trip back to Germany with a man who would be pope.

German Interlude

After his years as provincial of the Argentinian Jesuits, Father Jorge Mario Bergoglio (b. 1936) came to Germany to earn a doctorate in sacred theology (STD) at the Jesuit philosophical-theological college of Sankt Georgen, Frankfurt am Main, under the direction of Father Michael Sievernich, S.J. The topic should have been "Polar Opposition as Structure of

---

[1] Romano Guardini, *The Spirit of the Liturgy*, trans. Ada Lane (1998), in Joseph Cardinal Ratzinger, *The Spirit of the Liturgy*, with Romano Guardini, *The Spirit of the Liturgy*, Commemorative edition (San Francisco: Ignatius Press, 2018), 358.

Daily Thought and Christian Proclamation"—also on the primacy of *Logos* over *Ethos*, inspired by the title of the final chapter of Guardini's classic and by Father Sievernich's philosophical text *Der Gegensatz* (The opposition).[2] It seems Pope Francis joins other thinkers like Guardini in opposing Hegelian dialectics (where a resolution replaces two opposites) in favor of a Catholic "maintaining tensions"—as it was put succinctly by Saint John Henry Newman (1801–1890). Both Francis and Newman favor reconciling theological tension in a way that does not resolve friction in favor of one pole or eliminate polarities altogether. In this final chapter of his *The Spirit of the Liturgy*, Guardini holds the following positions:

1. It is only with the eyes of God, from the perspective of the Blessed Trinity, that everything in this world receives its proper valence and dignity.
2. Created in the image of God, but in a postlapsarian state, man must continually make the ethical effort to behold the world as divinely willed; and, therefore,
3. The Christian is obligated not only to resist but also to combat all forms of self-enamored immanentism (i.e., God's exclusive abiding in the world).

---

[2] Hannelore Crolly, "Bergoglio studierte einst in Frankfurt am Main," *Welt*, March 14, 2013, http://www.welt.de/politik/deutschland/article114452124 /Bergoglio-studierte-einst-in-Frankfurt-am-Main.html; Romano Guardini, *Der Gegensatz. Versuche zu einer Philosophie des lebendig Konkreten* (1955; Mainz: Matthias Grünewald, 1991).

This final accord as it applies to questions of the liturgy is translated in the book's last chapter head as "The Primacy of Logos over Ethos". Like Guardini, Bergoglio the doctoral candidate seems to perceive an underlying tension between these two key terms. Unfortunately, Bergoglio's doctoral project never materialized. On the occasion of *The Spirit of the Liturgy*'s centenary, though, it is fitting to reconsider Guardini's closing argument. Not only may it shed some light on the thinking of Pope Francis, who also approaches matters of faith, and especially of the liturgy, with a tension-filled polarity of dialectics, but such a study will also illuminate the essence—the spirit—of the liturgy, our principal goal.

Come Together

In Guardini's writings, every word is carefully weighed and considered and graced with a special *timbre*. This renders his writings inimitable and thus irreplaceable. He commonly refrains from arguing against another thinker, but rather—in the manner of true classic authors—intends to distill what is abidingly relevant and prevailing despite the vicissitudes of history.

Guardini begins the chapter by registering the regret many express for Catholic liturgy's apparent unrelatedness to current affairs and practical matters of daily life. (When using the term "liturgy", Guardini consistently means the Eucharist, the Catholic Holy Mass.)

Indeed, he emphasizes, liturgy resists being translated into action. These well-intended critiques are the occasion for him to develop the danger of allowing "outcomes" to determine the nature and purpose of liturgy. While not dwelling on the eminently doxological nature of man and the cosmos, he reminds his readers that "liturgy ... is primarily occupied in forming the fundamental Christian temper."[3] He does not deny that worship impacts the moral order. However, this is a necessary secondary consequence, not its purpose.

To establish the proper frame of reference for the tension between *Logos* and *Ethos*, Guardini points out that in the Christian Middle Ages primacy was given to the *Logos* vis-à-vis *Ethos*. The human will and its attendant activities were perceived during the Middle Ages as formed by and, therefore, the natural outgrowths of the *Logos*. Not only does the *Logos* chronologically precede all human activities, it also ontologically undergirds human action—and liturgical action. Provocatively, the "truth is truth because it is truth",[4] irrespective of what the will may interject, and therefore serves as the basis for *Ethos*. To this end, Guardini sees the rich devotional lives of Catholics, such as praying the rosary, meditations, processions, etc., as felicitous appropriations and incorporations of the *Logos* into the concrete and personal lives of the

---

[3] Guardini, *Spirit of the Liturgy*, 353.
[4] Ibid., 359.

faithful. (Guardini would pen precious meditations on the Stations of the Cross in 1921.)[5]

Holding *Logos* as the foundation for *Ethos* granted medieval society a historically unparalleled and singular cohesion and solidarity, enabling it to be more than a pragmatic commonwealth, but one of a shared meaning and thus shared destiny. The foundational *Logos* spelled out the nature of *Gemeinschaft* (community) versus merely *Gesellschaft* (society) and was expressed in a lasting manner in works of art. For instance, this position found visible expression in Italy's medieval municipal *Signorias* (city halls) adorned with saints and making no distinction between sacred and secular realms, just as today, of course, this shared meaning becomes ever again present in the liturgy: the Eucharist as the Thou of God in Jesus Christ—divinity appearing in the common accidents of bread and wine. (Guardini further develops this dimension on a broad canvas in *The Lord* years later.)[6]

We're Breaking Up

But following the Middle Ages, as the positive sciences ascended from the Renaissance onward, "the

[5] Romano Guardini, *Der Kreuzweg unseres Herrn und Heilandes* (Mainz: Matthias Grünewald, 1921).

[6] Romano Guardini, *The Lord*, trans. Elinor Castendyk Briefs (1937; Washington, D.C.: Regnery, 2002).

fulcrum of the spiritual life gradually shift[s] from knowledge [of the Divine] to [man's subjectively formed] will",[7] now perceived as autonomous and at best defined exclusively by verifiable, empirical criteria. As a result of this shifting emphasis from *Logos* to *Ethos*, from truth to action, our age is "a powerful, restlessly productive, laboring community".[8] Modernity has lost sight of a vital component of existence: listening to and obeying the inner order of being. "Contemplation of God or ... love of him"[9] is no longer deemed foundational to minds formed in primarily practical matters. Guardini is thinking here not only of the large, dehumanizing factories, such as those found in the grand modern metropolises of Berlin, Paris, or London, that result in massified individuals. He is also thinking of the ideas that generated these inhuman work centers, especially those of Friedrich Nietzsche's *The Will to Power*.[10] Guardini considered the work puerile, if not pathological and benighted—although today, tellingly, it is much read by the Western intelligentsia. Guardini asserts already for this age and time that "the Ethos has complete precedence over the Logos."[11]

---

[7] Guardini, *Spirit of the Liturgy*, 354.

[8] Ibid., 355.

[9] Ibid., 354n2.

[10] Friedrich Nietzsche, *The Will to Power: An Attempted Transvaluation of All Values*, vols. 1 and 2 (Boston, Mass.: Digireads, 2010), originally published posthumously in 1901.

[11] Guardini, *Spirit of the Liturgy*, 357.

Will and Kant

But we need to take a step even farther back in the history of German philosophy to understand how this usurpation of the primacy given to *Logos* by *Ethos* was prepared decades earlier than Nietzsche by the German philosopher Immanuel Kant. His philosophy of epistemological reticence (i.e., elevating human willing over knowing) is the logical conclusion of Lutheran sixteenth-century anthropology, which grants human nature *per se* nothing positive in the order of salvation. For Luther and Kant were in agreement that truth can no longer be perceived as of value apart from criteria distilled wholly from the immanent order. For Luther and Kant, too, faith thus becomes the child of the will and no longer resting on knowledge of truth. After all, Kant sees dogma as incapable of informing what human nature is. Indeed, for Kant, dogma is a superstitious position that must gradually retreat into the dustbins of history as human reason irresistibly expands our horizon of possible knowledge. Then, invariably we come to worship success. Yet, the content of success is defined independently from the Creator. Such is the "New World". "The practical will is everywhere the decisive factor," Guardini writes, "and the Ethos has complete precedence over the Logos, the active side of life over the contemplative."[12] Even liturgy

[12] Ibid.

in the modern world becomes a practical, results-based activity.

Catholicism's position in this regard must be always diametrically opposed to such a world view, as the Church is *the* vessel containing divine revelation, thus illuminating to man both his and the world's purpose. To this end, Guardini calls for a return to a Christ-centered understanding of reality—a *Logos*-centered view—one that can only benefit the liturgy and souls encountering Christ in the liturgy. Indeed, the Second Vatican Council spells out Guardini's Christocentrism with a celebrated line in *Gaudium et spes*: "The truth is that only in the mystery of the incarnate Word does the mystery of man take on light."[13] Were the Council Fathers then mindful of Guardini's observations? If they were not, it was at least clear that Guardini expresses and even anticipates the conciliar mind of the Church on this matter.

As stated, Guardini sees Protestantism as catalyst and representative of the posture that prioritizes *Ethos* over *Logos*. This posture stands in stark relief to the Church's more inclusive view of *Logos* and *Ethos* as a tension held, especially in the liturgy, in proper order. Guardini's contemporary Adolf von Harnack (1851–1930), the premier Protestant theologian of the day, had drafted Kaiser Wilhelm II's declaration

---

[13] Vatican Council II, Pastoral Constitution on the Church in the Modern World *Gaudium et spes* (December 7, 1965), 22.

of war in 1914. Did this bring into prominent focus for Guardini the foundational weakness of Protestant theology? Guardini sees Kant rightly "called [Protestant theology's] philosopher". Guardini writes that the Kantian spirit "has step by step abandoned objective religious truth, and has increasingly tended to make conviction a matter of personal judgment, feeling, and experience.... The relation with the supertemporal and eternal order is thereby broken."[14]

Consequently, in the Kantian and Lutheran line of thought, Scripture, dogmatizations, and liturgy are not inspired products of salvation history flowing from the decisive moment of Christ's death and Resurrection and giving expression to eternal truth; rather, these elements in the life of faith are entirely immanent events, subject to revision. Here the Faustian temptation to make the Deed the first word of salvation becomes a frightening realty.

Bargaining Souls

But even World War I was only a prelude to the twentieth-century fascination with this temptation. Hardly twenty years after the end of this first war to end all wars, the *Ethos* became all-dominant during the ugly works and days of the Nazi Third Reich. In

---

[14] Guardini, *Spirit of the Liturgy*, 357–58.

reaction to this ugliness, the world heralded a 1960 German film version of Goethe's *Faust*. The critics reserved special praise for the German actor Gustav Gründgens' stellar performance as Mephisto, the demon tempter and beguiling protagonist who urges Faust (and, the German audience might say, Hitler) to embrace the primacy of *Ethos*. Shortly after the film was released, however, Gründgens died—possibly by suicide. The irony would not have been lost on either Goethe or Guardini: man is utterly unable to live a life "unrestrained" by the *Logos*.[15]

Guardini argues positively that the rejection of the Catholic, magisterial claim to the primacy of *Logos* leads to "the position of a blind person groping his way in the dark, because the fundamental force upon which it has based life—the will—is [now] blind. The will can function and produce but cannot see. From this is derived the restlessness that nowhere finds tranquillity."[16] As we will see, this restlessness finds rest in a will guided through prayer in the liturgy.

This situation is also intensified in postmodernity, wherein the individual constantly and breathlessly performs and consumes and knows of no home. He seeks in temporality a transcendental meaning, which must remain elusive, but for this reason postmodernity offers incentives to invent more consumer goods.

[15] Ibid., 358.
[16] Ibid., 359.

Both performance and free time are placed under the dictatorship of the *Ethos*. Leisure, a cousin of the liturgy, becomes a frightful perspective that needs to be avoided at all costs, lest one need confront the truth of being, the *Logos*. In the ductus of Guardini's *The Spirit of Liturgy*, Josef Pieper (1904–1997) writes *Leisure: The Basis of Culture* (1948)[17] and Hugo Rahner (1900–1968) pens *Man at Play* (1952).[18] Do both Pieper and Hugo Rahner feel inspired especially by this last chapter of *The Spirit of Liturgy*? Human contemplation is but a retracing of a truth contained in things, which is a cognitive retracing of God's thoughts.

Life in a Word

Logos, the Word, is apprehended as one constantly effected by God and not a merely impersonal process. The things in this world bear its meaning and message. The primacy of the *Logos* allows for spontaneity both on God's side and on our side. Influenced by Bonaventure and with numerous fellow thinkers, Guardini shares skepticism as regards rigid systems and theoretical presentations. But Guardini is doing nothing more than the Church has always done. Catholicism has always resisted the temptation to reduce

---

[17] Josef Pieper, *Leisure: The Basis of Culture* (San Francisco: Ignatius Press, 2009).

[18] Hugo Rahner, *Man at Play* (New York: Herder and Herder, 1972).

metaphysics, truth, and dogma to ethical conceptions and to be guided by moral or pragmatic considerations divorced from a grounding in the divine. Cultic worship is similarly far more than education of the individual to be a good citizen à la the Enlightenment. We may become better citizens for going to Mass, but that is not the *primary* purpose of the divine liturgy. In this context, Guardini reminds the reader that even God as the Blessed Trinity, far from being impersonal or cerebral, is never merely an absolute will "but, at the same time, truth and goodness".[19] In this way, the Trinity is also the perfect model for the liturgy. The triune God is a constant living out of personal relationships of mutual commitment in love.

With Augustine, Guardini understands this charity as the Holy Spirit. Thus, the Blessed Trinity is perceived as the template for man and society. Is this "Augustinian interiority" what Pope Francis intended to demonstrate in his dissertation project? A community grounded in the incarnate God formed for Guardini the basis for the anti-Nazi activists Hans and Sophie Scholl's sacrifice of life in 1943. Guardini honors the witness of this community when he writes that it "lived in the radiance of Christ's sacrifice ... issuing forth from the creative origin of eternal love".[20] The incarnate *Logos*, Jesus Christ, is the enabler of human

---

[19] Guardini, *Spirit of the Liturgy*, 359n5.

[20] Romano Guardini, *Die Waage des Daseins* (Tübingen/Stuttgart: Wunderlich, 1946), 18: "obedience vis-à-vis the interior call".

charity and participation in divine vivacity. And even as this divine love was a harmonizing principle of word and act for the Scholls, so too it will always be, and more so, in the Catholic liturgy.

Word and Deed

The epochal process of depersonalization that the twenty-first-century countenances may be seen as the consequence of giving *Ethos* priority over and against *Logos*. But it would be incorrect to assume action is of inferior value to contemplation. It is the *Logos* that dignifies action, i.e., transforms all action into *Ethos* beyond compare.

Therefore, *Logos* and *Ethos* are not two entities that must be inexorably cancelled out in an immanent process for a higher third to emerge (à la Hegel's dialectical understanding of history). Neither can the claim be made that knowledge is more important than life. Rather, Guardini writes, "[i]t is partly a question of disposition; the tone of a man's life will accentuate either knowledge or action; and the one type of disposition is worth as much as the other ...; in life as a whole, precedence belongs, not to action, but to existence. What ultimately matters is not activity, but development"[21]—a reflected and deliberate growth

---

[21] Guardini, *Spirit of the Liturgy*, 360–61.

toward eternity, a growth that is at once human and informed by the divine life of grace.

At this point the question arises: What kind of thing is *Logos*? Guardini asks "whether truth insists upon love or upon frigid majesty".[22] *Ethos* on its own subjugates us to an impersonal, Kantian "obligation of the law" as defined by Kant's *The Postulates of Practical Reason*; but Guardini responds that *Logos* evokes "the obligation of creative love".[23] But this is not a complete answer to the question, either. Rather, with the Johannine Christ he argues that the "good news"[24] announces nothing less than that love is the greatest. The personal truth of the Thou of God "will make you free" (Jn 8:32) from the burden to justify human existence via tangible, human criteria. Jesus Christ shines forth, not as the final arbiter between *Logos* and *Ethos*, but as that singular reality that provides the proper equilibrium between the two, an equilibrium fully displayed in the harmony of the *Logos* and *Ethos* of the liturgy.

"In dogma, the fact of absolute truth, inflexible and eternal, entirely independent of a basis of practicality," Guardini writes, "we possess something that is inexpressibly great. When the soul becomes aware of it, it is overcome by a sensation as of having touched the mystic guarantee of universal sanity; it perceives

[22] Ibid., 361.
[23] Ibid.
[24] Ibid.

dogma as the guardian of all existence, actually and really the rock upon which the universe rests. 'In the beginning was the Word'—the Logos...."[25] In this way, Guardini responds to Goethe's Mephisto and suggests a restoration of the balance that the modern has lost.

Because that "guarantee of universal sanity" is so necessary for human existence, Guardini considers contemplation indispensable to genuine freedom. There is the call for man to ponder eternity to comprehend the eternal nature of his soul. "It is peaceful", Guardini writes, "it has that interior restraint which is a victory over life" for the sake of life.[26] For this reason, the Catholic faith, he notes, cannot "join in the furious pursuit of the unchained will, torn from its fixed and eternal order".[27]

Rather, the personal *Logos*, Jesus Christ, establishes a harmony that does not eliminate *Ethos* but provides its sure grounding in the order of being. "In the liturgy, the Logos has been assigned its fitting precedence over the will", Guardini states. In the accompanying footnote, he adds: "Because it reposes upon existence, upon the essential, and even upon existence *in* love...."[28] Man's purpose is contemplation, adoration, and glorification of divine truth. "The liturgy

[25] Ibid., 362.
[26] Ibid.
[27] Ibid.
[28] Ibid., 363 and n. 8 (emphasis added).

has something in itself reminiscent of the stars, of their eternally fixed and even course, of their inflexible order, of their profound silence, and of the infinite space in which they are poised."[29] In *The Spirit of the Liturgy*, Guardini thankfully provides a map to these stars, poised between the word and the deed, the *Logos* and the *Ethos*.

[29] Ibid., 363.

AFTERWORD

What Became of the Spirit of the Liturgy?

Susan Benofy

Considering that so much of the debate about liturgy today is concerned with the rite of Mass itself—Ordinary vs. Extraordinary Form, or the merits of proposed changes in the rite—the following statement from a book by Joseph Cardinal Ratzinger (Pope Emeritus Benedict XVI) may be surprising: "The crisis in the liturgy (and hence in the Church) in which we find ourselves has very little to do with the change from the old to the new liturgical books.... [T]here is a profound disagreement about the very nature of the liturgical celebration.... The basic concepts of the new view are creativity, freedom, celebration and community."[1]

Possibly more surprising is that proponents of the "new view" make similar statements. For example,

---

[1] Joseph Ratzinger, *Feast of Faith: Approaches to a Theology of Liturgy*, trans. Graham Harrison (San Francisco: Ignatius Press, 1980), 61.

liturgist Ralph Keifer said, "Considered from the perspective of the official texts, liturgical reform has meant only a modest revision of the Roman rite mass.... Yet this modest change of ceremony has helped to precipitate a revolution in our ritual."[2]

But if changes in the rite did not cause the "revolution", what did? In his remarks to the Roman Curia in 2005, Pope Benedict XVI spoke of larger interpretive conflicts concerning the Second Vatican Council. "The problems in its implementation", he said, "arose from the fact that two contrary hermeneutics came face to face and quarreled with each other. One caused confusion, the other, silently but more and more visibly, bore and is bearing fruit." The first, a "hermeneutic of discontinuity and rupture", saw sharp contrasts between the tradition and the postconciliar Church, invoking a so-called "spirit of the council" divorced from the actual texts of the council. The second hermeneutic, one of "reform and renewal", read the conciliar texts and the postconciliar reform in continuity with what came before, even while adapting ecclesial life, when and where possible, to modern conditions.

The liturgy—in its practice, its theology, and its spirit—similarly succumbed to battling hermeneutics.

---

[2] Ralph A. Keifer, *The Mass in Time of Doubt: The Meaning of the Mass for Catholics Today* (Washington, D.C.: National Association of Pastoral Musicians, 1983), 56. Keifer was professor of liturgy at Catholic Theological Union in Chicago, acting executive secretary (1972–1973) and general editor (1971–1973) of the International Commission on English in the Liturgy (ICEL).

Changes wrought in the liturgy came about through a divergence in focus on what the liturgy essentially *is*. Two predominant views of the liturgy emerged after the council, and it is this divergence that has created the unhealthy tension that the faithful experience in "liturgical politics" even today. The first of these views, which is more sympathetic to tradition, holds that there is an objective pattern of worship that all liturgy embraces. The second is more subjective and holds that the liturgy is most perfectly realized when tailored to the communal experience of worship. Benedict and Kiefer both see the "spirit of liturgy"—be it objective or subjective—as the starting point of post-conciliar renewal. To appreciate the quarreling "spirits of the liturgy", and to appreciate what the Council Fathers themselves held it to be, we need not go back far in Church history to see that the objective view is the correct view.

Texts of the Council

Consider what the council itself, in its Constitution on the Sacred Liturgy (*Sacrosanctum concilium* [*SC*]), saw as crucial to liturgical reform: "In the restoration and promotion of the sacred liturgy, this full and active participation by all the people is the aim to be considered before all else; for it is the primary and indispensable source from which the faithful are to derive the true Christian spirit.... Yet it would be futile to entertain any hopes of realizing this unless the pastors themselves, in the first place, become thoroughly imbued with the spirit and power of the liturgy, and undertake to give instruction about it" (*SC*, 14).

Though the earlier parts of paragraph 14 are quoted in virtually every discussion of liturgical reform, the second sentence above is rarely cited, even though the constitution is quite emphatic here.

The council did not give specific details about what constituted this true "spirit of the liturgy". The phrase had appeared in Pope Pius XI's 1928 apostolic constitution *Divini cultus* and in Pope Pius XII's 1948 encyclical letter *Mediator Dei*. The expression also brings to mind two books of that title. The more recent, a 2000 book by Cardinal Ratzinger,[3] was inspired by Romano Guardini's 1918 book of the same name. Ratzinger says that Guardini's book *The Spirit of the Liturgy* "inaugurated the Liturgical Movement in Germany. Its contribution was decisive. It helped us to rediscover the liturgy in all its beauty ... and time-transcending grandeur ... as the prayer of the Church, ... guided by the Holy Spirit himself...."[4]

---

[3] Joseph Cardinal Ratzinger, *The Spirit of the Liturgy*, trans. John Saward (2000), in Joseph Cardinal Ratzinger, *The Spirit of the Liturgy*, with Romano Guardini, *The Spirit of the Liturgy*, Commemorative edition (San Francisco: Ignatius Press, 2018).

[4] Ibid., 21.

Since it is generally agreed that the liturgical movement, in turn, influenced the council's reform of the liturgy, it seems reasonable to take Guardini's 1918 book as a guide to the spirit of the liturgy that *Sacrosanctum concilium* considered so crucial.

Objective Spirit

Guardini lays great stress on the slow development of the liturgy through time. Though influenced by a variety of cultures, it does not reflect any single one, but "is the supreme example of an objectively established rule of spiritual life". Furthermore, he states, "The primary and exclusive aim of the liturgy is not the expression of the individual's reverence and worship of God.... In the liturgy, God is to be honored by the body of the faithful.... It is important that this objective nature of the liturgy should be fully understood."[5] As a consequence of this objectivity, the liturgy "is a school of religious training and development to the Catholic who rightly understands it".[6]

However, Guardini also says, the liturgy is difficult to adapt to modern man, who often finds it artificial and too formal and prefers other forms of prayer

[5] Romano Guardini, *The Spirit of the Liturgy*, trans. Ada Lane (1998), in Ratzinger, *Spirit of the Liturgy*, 277–78.
[6] Ibid., 309–10.

that seem to have the advantage "of contemporary or, at any rate, of congenial origin".[7] But to be appropriate as a prayer for all people and any situation, the liturgy must be formal and keep "emotion under the strictest control".[8]

The direct expression of emotion in prayer is more appropriate in personal prayer or popular devotions. These are rightly intended to appeal to certain tastes and circumstances and, consequently, retain more local characteristics and aim more at individual edification, but they must remain distinct from the liturgy. "There could be no greater mistake than that of discarding the valuable elements in the spiritual life of the people for the sake of the liturgy or than the desire of assimilating them to it."[9] The liturgy is celebrated by the whole body of the faithful, not simply the assembled congregation. It embraces "all the faithful on earth. Simultaneously it reaches beyond the bounds of time."[10]

Guardini notes that, since the liturgy does not fit any personality type exactly, all must sacrifice some of their own inclinations to enter into it properly. And, though liturgy requires fellowship, this does not mean ordinary social interaction. "[T]he union of the members is not directly accomplished from man to man. It

---

[7] Ibid., 310.
[8] Ibid., 285.
[9] Ibid., 279.
[10] Ibid., 297.

is accomplished by and in their joint aim, goal, and spiritual resting place—God—by their identical creed, sacrifice and sacraments."[11] Guardini insists that liturgical prayer "must spring from the fullness of truth. It is only truth—or dogma, to give it its other name—that can make prayer efficacious."[12]

Revolutionary Spirit

Now consider how the "revolution" in the liturgy was brought about. According to Keifer: "The real revolution was that the agents of reform ... effectively abolished the distinction between sanctuary and nave."[13] They relocated "the place of the holy in the midst of the assembly",[14] placing the people—not God—at the center of the liturgy and shifting the focus of prayer. Kiefer claims that "liturgical prayer is not simply speech in common addressed to God. Rather, it is speech to one another addressed in God's 'overhearing.'"[15]

Who were these "agents of reform" Keifer mentions? Many were speakers and writers, associated with liturgical publications and organizations, especially

[11] Ibid., 303.
[12] Ibid., 281.
[13] Keifer, *Mass in Time of Doubt*, 56.
[14] Ibid., 65.
[15] Ibid., 87.

the Liturgical Conference. This organization was very influential around the time of the council through its publications, annual conferences (called Liturgical Weeks), and numerous workshops.[16] A series of books, *The Parish Worship Program*,[17] was planned the very week that *Sacrosanctum concilium* was approved by the council, and, according to its then president, Father Gerard Sloyan, the series was designed to communicate the change in spirit that he believed was the most important impending change in the liturgy. Two prominent members of the Liturgical Conference were Father (later Monsignor) Frederick McManus, who served several terms as its president, and Father Godfrey Diekmann, O.S.B. (of Saint John's Abbey in Collegeville, Minnesota), a member of the conference's board and a frequent speaker at Liturgical Weeks.[18] They gave many talks on *Sacrosanctum concilium*, especially for priests, between sessions of

[16] For more on the Liturgical Conference, see Susan Benofy, "The Day the Mass Changed–Part I", *Adoremus Bulletin*, February 2010. A very large number of people participated in the workshops. In Chicago alone, "an initial six-week training program for commentators, lectors, and leaders of song involved no less than 11,400 laymen." See Godfrey Diekmann, O.S.B., "Liturgical Practice in the United States and Canada", in *Concilium: Theology in the Age of Renewal*, vol. 12, *The Church Worships* (Glen Rock, N.J.: Paulist Press, 1966), 164.

[17] These books were said to be "the first and for a long time the only aids made available to guide the celebration in the new rites". See Gordon E. Truitt, "Gerard Sloyan: Bridge of the Spirit", in *How Firm a Foundation: Leaders of the Liturgical Movement*, compiled and introduced by Robert L. Tuzik (Chicago: Liturgy Training publications, 1990), 222–99. See especially 295.

[18] Both served as liturgical *periti* (experts) at Vatican II and were long-term members of the ICEL Advisory Committee. McManus was also the first director of the Secretariat of the Bishops' Committee on the Liturgy (1965–1975).

the council.[19] Others in this chapter include Clement
McNaspy, S.J., another board member of the Liturgical Conference, and Father Robert Hovda of Fargo,
North Dakota, editor of its publications from 1965
to 1978.[20] The contrast between this "new spirit"
expressed in their work and Guardini's is striking.

One revolutionary change in spirit is already evident in a 1963 book of essays, *Sunday Morning Crisis:
Renewal in Catholic Worship*, which proclaimed on
its cover: "Here, for the first time, is what liturgical renewal means to you."[21] In his introduction,
Father Hovda asserts, like Keifer, that liturgy is primarily communal and only secondarily a matter of
the worship owed to God: "[I]t is through relating
to one another before God ... that Christians properly worship and accomplish the proper purpose of
worship. The following essays hope to help make
that relating a matter of common Sunday morning
experience."[22]

[19] In a letter to J.B. O'Connell dated March 3, 1964, Diekmann wrote:
"Fred [McManus] and I have been very busy lecturing to groups of priests
throughout the country ever since returning from Rome. And the list of such
engagements stretches through the next months, until September. Actually,
it has been very edifying to discover how willing, and even eager, priests of
advanced years are to listen and to learn. If only we can reach enough of them."
Quoted in Kathleen Hughes, R.S.C.J., *The Monk's Tale: A Biography of Godfrey
Diekmann, O.S.B.* (Collegeville, Minn.: Liturgical Press, 1991), 252.
[20] Hovda was also principal author of the U.S. Bishops' Committee on the
Liturgy 1978 statement "Environment and Art in Catholic Worship". McNaspy
was a musicologist and an editor of the Jesuit magazine *America*.
[21] Robert Hovda, ed., *Sunday Morning Crisis: Renewal in Catholic Worship*
(Baltimore: Helicon Press, 1963) (imprimatur dated July 17, 1963).
[22] Robert Hovda, Introduction, *Sunday Morning Crisis*, 4 (original emphasis).

Likewise, McManus, in his essay in this volume,[23] claims that during the first session of Vatican II the Council Fathers approved a liturgical reform based on three principles: the communal nature of the liturgy, its pastoral purpose, and its adaptability. (Note how closely these correspond to Cardinal Ratzinger's description of the "new view".) The pastoral purpose, McManus says, means that changes in the liturgy will be dictated by the needs of the people and can no longer conform to a universal pattern that looks first to the proper objective worship of God. Therefore, since there is a great diversity of cultures in the world, the liturgy "must match this diversity and be open, always open, to change and growth.... Times and customs change, so must the ways of worship."[24]

But the emphasis on direct communication between people "radically *localizes* the liturgy", as Keifer pointed out. Local languages and styles of music replace worldwide use of Latin and Gregorian chant, for example. "This contributes effectively to a fading of the Roman, and hence, the papal image that the liturgy once carried. This is the reason why appeals to outside authority about details of practice are experienced as so incongruous and inappropriate now."[25]

In addition, this emphasis on the local produces the very situation Guardini warned against: the loss of

---

[23] Frederick McManus, "What Is Being Done?" in Hovda, *Sunday Morning Crisis*, 45–58.

[24] Ibid., 55.

[25] Keifer, *Mass in Time of Doubt*, 60.

the necessary distinction between liturgy and devotions. In fact, contrary to *Sacrosanctum concilium*,[26] these liturgists scorned devotions, anticipating their disappearance. Even Eucharistic devotions will decline, McManus predicts in an essay in the 1963 volume *The Revival of the Liturgy*: "With the devotion of the people now directed to the eucharistic meal, the accidentals in the Eucharistic cult outside Mass will not flourish so widely."[27]

In contrast to the gradual development of the liturgy in the past, and ignoring the council's call for "careful investigation ... into each part of the liturgy which is to be revised" (*SC* 23), these liturgists were in a great hurry to implement their views. In fact, McManus insists that "progressives" must not compromise but "must take more advanced positions from the beginning ... to leave room for concession or bargain."[28] "If too little is sought or attempted, doors now open may be shut."[29]

---

[26] "Popular devotions of the Christian people are to be highly commended, provided they accord with the laws and norms of the Church.... But these devotions should be so drawn up that they harmonize with the liturgical seasons, accord with the Sacred Liturgy, are in some fashion derived from it, and lead the people to it...."

[27] Frederick McManus, "The Future: Its Hope and Difficulties", in *The Revival of the Liturgy*, ed. Frederick R. McManus (New York: Herder and Herder, 1963), 209 (imprimatur August 8, 1963).

[28] Ibid., 212–13.

[29] Ibid., 218. Yet as late as 2004, McManus, though regretting that recent Vatican documents had narrowed "the openness of the great council to adaptation and inculturation", still asserted "no door has been closed." See *Pastoral Music*, October–November 2004: 45–47.

Premature Interpretation

Both *Sunday Morning Crisis* and *The Revival of the Liturgy* have *imprimaturs* dating from the summer of 1963, before the second session of Vatican II had even begun. So these essays interpreted *Sacrosanctum concilium* before it was eventually promulgated on December 4, 1963, or even fully discussed at the council. Implementing "advanced positions" arguably changed people's *experience* of the liturgy (as the liturgists intended) more than the changes actually authorized by *Sacrosanctum concilium* and the earliest implementing documents. Directing the focus of the liturgy to the assembly, they tended to desacralize the liturgy.

In a 1964 essay, Father McNaspy notes that all known religions distinguish between the sacred and the profane. The sacred is "*apart*, separate.... The holy is what one does not touch, does not discuss, often ... does not even pronounce."[30] But since in modern times we stress rationality over mystery, he cautions against "too casual an acceptance of the terms 'sacral' or 'holy'"[31] and rejects the traditional forms that express it. For example, Romanesque and Gothic architecture and Gregorian chant are, he admits, "apart" today. But instead of considering these ancient forms, as Guardini does, to be part of a gradually developing objective

[30] Clement J. McNaspy, S.J., "The Sacral in Liturgical Music", in McManus, *Revival of the Liturgy*, 163–90. See particularly page 166.
[31] Ibid., 167.

pattern, McNaspy associates them exclusively with the past and believes their use today is actually a danger: "Does it not suggest that religion is simply quaint, archaic, and irrelevant?"[32]

Diekmann also rejects traditional forms of architecture in an essay on this subject. Although not published until 1965, it is clear from the text that the essay was written before September 1964 in anticipation of the Vatican instructions on the arrangement of churches found in *Inter oecumenici*. Diekmann even admits that it may seem premature to offer details, as he does, before the official document is promulgated. But he believes his procedure is justified since he intends simply to "draw what seem reasonable deductions from the *altiora principia* ('higher principles') contained in the Constitution".[33] He argues that *ecclesia*, meaning church, was first applied exclusively to the assembly and only later to the church building: "The *ecclesia*, as worshiping People of God, most effectively manifesting the infinite mystery of the Church, ranks among the *altiora principia* of the Constitution."[34] From this

[32] Ibid., 178.

[33] Godfrey Diekmann, O.S.B., "The Place of Liturgical Worship", in *Concilium: Theology in the Age of Renewal*, vol. 2, *The Church and the Liturgy* (Glen Rock, N.J.: Paulist Press, 1965), 67–107. See particularly page 68. He does not specify where in *Sacrosanctum concilium* he finds these higher principles. If, in fact, the suggestions he makes in this essay depend on *SC*, it is odd that they were already featured in a church built in the 1950s: the Abbey Church of Saint John's, which Diekmann helped to plan. See Hughes, *Monk's Tale*, 169–75.

[34] Diekmann, "Place of Liturgical Worship", 73–74.

he concludes that the primary purpose of a church building is to facilitate the "common experience of community".[35]

Consequently, he insists that churches must not be "grandiose 'monuments to God's glory,' "[36] but rather designed so that each person can experience "a meaningful function in the common action. This would unquestionably rule out the long rectangle, the one shape of a church that has been most customary."[37]

He also interprets a second higher principle—emphasis on the Paschal mysteries—as requiring personal and communal experience. This can be facilitated, he suggests, by a standing posture after the Consecration and during the reception of Holy Communion. Since he believes that the Communion rail "has come to connote ... a wall of separation from the sanctuary", he recommends distribution to standing communicants at Communion "stations" as "paradoxically, both more reverent and swift".[38] He also believes the altar should be free-standing with the priest facing the people. Visually obstructive objects, including the crucifix, should be removed. As to other images, he tells us: "it may be 'the better part' for the present to be prudently and orthodoxally iconoclastic."[39]

[35] Ibid., 75.
[36] Ibid., 76.
[37] Ibid., 85.
[38] Ibid., 98.
[39] Ibid., 105.

The Vatican's instruction, entitled *Inter oecumenici*, when it was promulgated on September 26, 1964, lacked many of the provisions Diekmann anticipated. It did provide that the main altar "should *preferably* be free-standing to *permit* celebration facing the people" (*IO* 91, emphasis added). It spoke of the "cross and candlesticks *required* on the altar" (*IO* 94, emphasis added). It said nothing about removing the Communion rail, standing for Holy Communion, or the need for the church building to facilitate the experience of community.

Even though Diekmann's 1964 predictions so often went beyond, or even contradicted, the subsequently released *Inter oecumenici*, McManus praised Diekmann's essay in a 1965 address to 500 architects and church building commission members. Diekmann was writing before the promulgation of the 1964 instruction, McManus said, but added that "it is valid now and will be as valuable in the future. The meaning of norms must be sought in the supporting reasons, for which we must look to the commentators."[40] While the instruction's norms may seem legalistic, McManus said, they allow "for the greatest creativity", aim "to restore the meaning of the Eucharist as community action", and recognize that "there should be diversity, adaptation

[40] Frederick McManus, "Recent Documents on Church Architecture", in *Church Architecture: The Shape of Reform: Proceedings of a Meeting on Church Architecture Conducted by the Liturgical Conference February 23–25, 1965, in Cleveland, Ohio* (Washington, D.C.: Liturgical Conference, 1965), 87.

to local circumstances and occasions."[41] That is, he insists this instruction supports the "new view".

Liturgical Changes

Inter oecumenici also included some changes in the rite of Mass. Among the most obvious were permission for vernacular recitation (or singing) of most prayers said by the people and priest (together or in dialogue) and the new formula for distributing Holy Communion (*Corpus Christi*). A few of the prayers said by the priest—formerly said in silence—were to be said aloud, and readings were proclaimed in the vernacular at a lectern facing the people. Laymen could read those scriptural selections before the priest proclaimed the Gospel. Some texts from the Mass were altogether omitted, such as Psalm 42 (from the Prayers at the Foot of the Altar), the Last Gospel (Jn 1:1–14), and the Leonine prayers recited after Mass by priest and people. There also were a few ceremonial changes concerning the sung Mass and incense.

In the United States, the instruction was implemented on November 29, 1964,[42] and that implementation should have entailed only the changes to the

---

[41] Ibid., 94–95.

[42] Not only was this interval between promulgation and implementation (September 2—November 29) quite short, but the bishops, who were to direct this implementation, were absent from their dioceses for most of it. They were in Rome attending the third session of the council, which ran almost exactly concurrent with this interval—from September 14 to November 21.

rite mentioned above. However, the optional practice of celebrating Mass facing the people became almost universal.[43] Visually, in accordance with the "new views" that Guardini sought to avoid and Pope Benedict roundly criticized, this tended to focus the liturgy on the people. The addition of receiving Communion standing, the removal of Communion rails and statues, as well as the singing of four vernacular hymns (none of which was even mentioned by the council or the instruction) tended to convey the "new spirit" and made the *experience* seem more like a "new liturgy" altogether.

The hymn-singing, however, was a continuation of a preconciliar practice that permitted hymns in the vernacular during a low (read) Mass.[44] The low Mass was the most common form before the council and was often preferred by influential liturgists for its "flexibility". The pattern of four hymns at low Mass was promoted particularly by the Liturgical Conference in the 1950s,[45] and its influential *Parish Worship Program*[46]

---

[43] In most places, this involved an arrangement not apparently envisioned by the 1964 instruction: placing a new table-style altar in the sanctuary in front of the old main altar. Since the new altar could appear insignificant contrasted with the older abandoned, but more impressive, main altar, this could seem to diminish the significance of the Mass.

[44] See the September 3, 1958, Instruction on Sacred Music and Sacred Liturgy from the Sacred Congregation for Rites, *De musica sacra et sacra liturgia*, 14b.

[45] See Eugene A. Walsh, S.S., "Making Active Participation Come to Life", in *People's Participation and Holy Week: 17th North American Liturgical Week* (Elsberry, Mo.: Liturgical Conference, 1957), 45–63.

[46] See the volume in this program: *A Manual for Church Musicians* (Washington, D.C.: Liturgical Conference, 1964), especially 47–50. See also Susan Benofy, "The Day the Mass Changed—Part II", *Adoremus Bulletin*, March 2010.

recommended this as the preferred form of Mass after the council. So, though singing by the people was emphasized and occurred at almost all Masses after the council, the sung (high) Mass, which required the singing of liturgical texts themselves, virtually disappeared.[47]

At first the hymns were fairly traditional, but soon they were replaced by a secular style of music. This development was promoted by Diekmann in an address to the annual convention of the National Catholic Education Association (NCEA) in April 1965. According to press reports, Diekmann "spelled out the task of teaching the Mass to students through participation geared to their way of communicating with each other".[48] Asking how teachers could help the Mass become "subjectively, in the thinking and living of our pupils ..., the fount of all holiness ...?" he answered: "Quite frankly, I wish I knew."[49] Yet he does not hesitate to make concrete suggestions.

[47] There was, in fact, an obstacle to having a sung Mass with English liturgical texts at this time. Melodies for texts to be sung by the priest or ministers required approval from the conference of bishops (see *Inter Oecumenici*, 42). Yet it was not until November 17, 1965, that the U.S. Bishops' Conference approved such settings, which could not be used until March 27, 1966. See *Thirty-Five Years of the BCL Newsletter 1965–2000* (Washington, D.C.: United States Conference of Catholic Bishops, 2004), 34.

[48] See, for example, in the diocesan paper of the Archdiocese of Indianapolis: "'Hootenanny Mass' Defended by Liturgist", *The Criterion*, May 14, 1965: 7.

[49] "Liturgical Renewal and the Student Mass" (an address delivered at the 62nd annual NCEA Convention, April 19–22, 1965), *Bulletin: National Catholic Education Association* 62, no. 1 (August 1965): 290–300. See particularly page 295.

Diekmann seems most concerned that students, allegedly impatient with formality, are bored at Mass, which *Sacrosanctum concilium* calls a "celebration". This word choice, he says, means it should be a "shared festivity", so he suggests that the "experiment and variety" allowed by the "new liturgy" be used to make the student Mass a "lived faith experience" and a "meaningful pleasure to be looked forward to". Contrary to Guardini's thoughts on the matter, Diekmann does not suggest that students learn to see the Mass as a "school of religious training", as Guardini explicitly says,[50] or that they be instructed in the Church's heritage of sacred music. Instead, students must have maximum input on the details of the Mass, including the music. He anticipates the sort of music the students will request, asking, "Are we perhaps sinning against our high-schoolers, depriving them of lawful celebration which, according to their culture ... would foster faith, if we exclude folk song [and] spirituals—or 'Kum 'ba Ya'?"[51] He implicitly answers in the affirmative by proposing what he calls the "hootenanny Mass" for student liturgies in high schools.

The audience of 3,000 Catholic educators, it was reported, responded to this talk with "thunderous applause".[52]

---

[50] Guardini, *Spirit of the Liturgy*, 309.

[51] Diekmann, "Liturgical Renewal and the Student Mass", 297.

[52] See "'Hootenanny Mass' Defended by Liturgist". About the same time, Father McNaspy promoted the "folk Mass" for college students. See "*America* Editor Defends 'Folk Mass'" on the same page in *The Criterion*, May 14, 1965.

That's All Folk!

Another enthusiast for the folk Mass, Ken Canedo, in his history *Keep the Fire Burning*,[53] traces the early development of liturgical "folk" music by Catholic composers (often seminarians) and the spread of this music (and the idea of congregational input) as it replaced more traditional hymns in schools and colleges throughout the country. This early folk-style music is often rightly criticized for its poor quality,[54] but rarely mentioned is the additional problem of the attitude and the "spirit" it introduced into the Mass.

Canedo notes that in the early twentieth century "folk music took root in the cities as a medium of radical thought." Some folk singers wrote original songs in folk style, which "directly challenged the establishment". This eventually "blossomed into the protest-laden radicalism" of the 1960s.[55] Consequently, Canedo writes, the folk Mass "sometimes became a worshipful act of defiance in dioceses that banned it".[56]

[53] Ken Canedo, *Keep the Fire Burning: The Folk Mass Revolution* (Portland, Ore.: Pastoral Press, 2009). There are podcasts that summarize the book and give samples of the compositions in it at https://kencanedo.com/podcasts. Canedo is currently a liturgical composer and music development specialist at Oregon Catholic Press.

[54] Yet it was performed at Carnegie Hall. Canedo explains that McNaspy organized a concert of liturgical "folk" music at this venue "to introduce to the public the new musical innovations going on in the Church at the time" (*Keep the Fire Burning*, 81). A live recording was made of this concert and released on LP. Some tracks from this recording can be heard on Canedo's podcast, "Chapter 9B".

[55] Canedo, *Keep the Fire Burning*, 18–19.

[56] Ibid., 72.

But the "establishment" being defied here was legitimate Church authority, and the defiance soon extended beyond worship. On January 31, 1966, the *New York Times* reported: "A group of University of Detroit students demonstrated yesterday in front of the Archdiocese of Detroit chancery against a ban of a folk-music-style Mass.... Some 50 students marched in freezing weather in front of the Chancery, carrying a sign: 'We want our Mass.' "[57]

This music (and the "new spirit") soon spread to parishes. Instead of the promised experience of community, however, it resulted in the division of the parish into factions, each saying, in effect: "We want our Mass."

Sense and Sentimentality

Guardini, decades before, had warned against these very approaches to the liturgy. Diekmann contended that liturgical participation would be enhanced by adaptations intended to increase personal pleasure. But Guardini considers this "sentimentality", i.e., "the desire to be moved", as an *obstacle* to participation. Adapting the Mass to the congregation's tastes blocks participation because the form of the Mass is "that which obedience to the Lord's command has received from His

[57] Ibid., 71, citing a *New York Times* article from February 1, 1966, "Detroit U Students Protest Ban of Folk-Music Mass".

Church.... He who really wishes to believe—in other words, to obey revelation—must obey also in this, schooling his private sentiments on that norm."[58]

Furthermore, Guardini warned that when a believer is no longer concerned with fundamental principles, but only with his own personal faith experience, "the one solid and recognizable fact is no longer a body of dogma ... but the right action as a proof of the right spirit.... Religion becomes increasingly turned toward the world and cheerfully secular."[59] Soon dogma itself became a matter of protest, most prominently in the reaction to *Humanae vitae* in 1968.

The council and earlier liturgical movement intended something very different from what the "new view" had in mind. On December 25, 1961, Pope John XXIII officially convoked the Second Vatican Council with the Apostolic Constitution *Humanae salutis*, in which he expressed the hope that the council "imbues with Christian light and penetrates with fervent spiritual energy not only into the depths of souls but also into the whole realm of human activities". Similarly, twenty-five years earlier, the American liturgical pioneer Virgil Michel, O.S.B., expected that a Christian who "drinks deep at the liturgical sources of the Christ-life" would "spare no effort to Christianize his environment", resulting in "a true

[58] Romano Guardini, *Meditations before Mass* (Manchester, N.H.: Sophia Institute Press, 2013), 101.
[59] Guardini, *Spirit of the Liturgy*, 357–58.

reflourishing of Christian culture, of the arts and literature, of social institutions formed after the mind of Christ".[60]

But today, as Gerhard Cardinal Müller, former Prefect of the Congregation of the Doctrine of the Faith, has recognized: "We are experiencing conversion to the world, instead of to God."[61] Why? Recall that the council itself told us that it "would be futile to entertain any hopes of realizing" the goal of active participation and liturgical renewal unless priests and people were first "thoroughly imbued with the spirit and power of the liturgy" (SC 14).

Spirit of the Liturgy Revisited

By the end of 1965, years before the Novus Ordo Missae was promulgated, only a few changes had been mandated for the rite itself. Yet the introduction of other practices not mentioned in Sacrosanctum concilium had already changed people's experience of the liturgy. They were designed to imbue priests and people with a "new spirit", contrary to the one Guardini

---

[60] Virgil Michel, O.S.B., "The Scope of the Liturgical Movement", Orate Fratres (Worship) 10 (1935–1936): 485–90. See particularly page 488. Michel was a monk of Saint John's Abbey in Collegeville, Minnesota, and the first editor of Orate Fratres.

[61] Gerhard Cardinal Müller in Catholic World Report, June 26, 2018, https://www.catholicworldreport.com/2018/06/26/cdl-muller-we-are-experiencing-conversion-to-the-world-instead-of-to-god/.

had proposed. Fifty years later, the liturgical reform has not reached its goal, and we experience ever more strongly what Cardinal Ratzinger called "the crisis in the liturgy (and hence in the Church)". This suggests that the new spirit was not what *Sacrosanctum concilium* 14 meant.

Reexamining postconciliar liturgical practices, guided by Guardini and *Sacrosanctum concilium*, would perhaps allow today's Catholics to become imbued with the true spirit of the liturgy as the council urged. Eliminating those practices not in accord with *Sacrosanctum concilium* and this spirit could help people to experience a time-transcending, beautiful liturgy as well as congregational unity that is not merely social but "is accomplished by and in their joint aim, goal, and spiritual resting place—God—by their identical creed, sacrifice, and sacraments".[62] And it would no longer be futile to hope, with Pope John XXIII, that through the restored liturgy, fervent spiritual energy would penetrate souls and lead to the transformation of the whole realm of human activities.

---

[62] Guardini, *Spirit of the Liturgy*, 303.

AUTHOR BIOS

Christopher Carstens *is editor of the* Adoremus Bulletin, *Director of the Office for Sacred Worship in the Diocese of La Crosse, Wisconsin, a visiting faculty member at the Liturgical Institute at the University of Saint Mary of the Lake in Mundelein, Illinois, and one of the voices on* The Liturgy Guys *podcast. He is author of* A Devotional Journey into the Mass *(Sophia) and* Principles of Sacred Liturgy: Forming a Sacramental Vision *(Hillenbrand). He lives in Soldiers Grove, Wisconsin, with his wife and eight children.*

Bishop Arthur Serratelli *has served as bishop of the Diocese of Paterson, New Jersey, since 2004. In November 2016, he concluded his term as Chairman of the U.S. Bishops' Committee on Divine Worship. In October 2016, he was appointed by Pope Francis as a member of the Holy See's Congregation for Divine Worship and the Discipline of the Sacraments. At present, he is the Chairman of the International Committee on English in the Liturgy (ICEL). He is also a member of the Vatican's Vox Clara Commission.*

Father Cassian Folsom, O.S.B., *is a scholar of sacred music and liturgy, a cancer survivor, and the founder and prior emeritus of the Monks of Norcia. Born in Lynn,*

Massachusetts, in 1955, Father Cassian studied music before joining the monastic community of Saint Meinrad in 1974. He founded his monastic community in Rome in 1998 and transferred it to Norcia in the year 2000. Over the last fifteen years, the Monastery di San Benedetto has grown, attracting new vocations and pilgrims from around the world. He recently retired as prior but continues to serve the community and teach liturgy at the Pontifical Liturgical Institute in Rome.

Dr. Michon Matthiesen *is Associate Professor at the University of Mary, Bismarck, North Dakota. Before arriving at the University of Mary, Dr. Matthiesen taught at Providence College (Rhode Island), Loyola Marymount University (California), and Saint Patrick's Seminary and University (California). Though rooted in the thought of Thomas Aquinas, she enjoys reading theologians of the early twentieth century who were keen to retrieve the rich and majestic thought of the early Church Fathers. Her oldest love, literature, led her to studies in liturgical and sacramental theology. Her book* Sacrifice as Gift: Eucharist, Grace, and Contemplative Prayer in Maurice de la Taille *urges a recovery of an understanding of Eucharistic sacrifice that is completed by a theology of grace and contemplative prayer. She has also written on the French school of spirituality, Flannery O'Connor, Thomas Aquinas, and Romano Guardini.*

David W. Fagerberg *is Professor in the Department of Theology at the University of Notre Dame. He holds an*

M.Div. from Luther Northwestern Seminary; an M.A. from Saint John's University, Collegeville; an S.T.M. from Yale Divinity School; and Ph.D. from Yale University. First, his work has explored how lex orandi *is the foundation for* lex credendi, *in* Theologia Prima *(2003). Second, to this he integrated the Eastern Orthodox understanding of asceticism as preparing the liturgical person in* On Liturgical Asceticism *(2013). Third, he has applied this to our liturgical life in the world in* Consecrating the World: On Mundane Liturgical Theology *(2016). He also has an avocation in G.K. Chesterton, having published* The Size of Chesterton's Catholicism *(1998) and* Chesterton Is Everywhere *(2013).*

Father Daniel Cardó was born in Lima, Peru, in 1975. A member of the Sodalitium Christianae Vitae, he was ordained to the priesthood in 2006 and in 2010 was appointed to Holy Name Parish, Denver. He received his doctorate from Maryvale Institute in 2015 and holds the Benedict XVI Chair for Liturgical Studies at Saint John Vianney Theological Seminary in Denver. He is also visiting professor at the Augustine Institute. He is the author of The Cross and the Eucharist in Early Christianity *(Cambridge University Press), a study on patristic and liturgical sources that offers a contribution for current liturgical debates; and of* What Does It Mean to Believe? *(Emmaus Academic), in which he explores Joseph Ratzinger's theology of faith.*

Originally ordained for the Diocese of Wichita, Kansas, in his years as a priest, the Most Reverend James D.

Conley *has served the Catholic Church in a wide variety of ways—as pastor, college campus chaplain, director of Respect Life ministries, theology instructor, and a Vatican official. On April 10, 2008, Pope Benedict XVI named him auxiliary bishop for the Archdiocese of Denver, and he was ordained on May 30, 2008. On September 14, 2012, Pope Benedict XVI appointed Bishop Conley as the ninth bishop of the Diocese of Lincoln in Nebraska. Bishop Conley was installed on November 20, 2012, in the Cathedral of the Risen Christ in Lincoln.*

Father Emery de Gaál *was born in Chicago but spent most of his life in Hungary and Bavaria. A priest of the Diocese of Eichstätt, Germany, Father de Gaál served in parishes and taught theology before Francis Cardinal George, O.M.I., called him to teach dogmatic theology at the University of Saint Mary of the Lake/Mundelein Seminary. His areas of concentration are medieval thought and Ressourcement theology, especially Anselm studies* (The Art of Equanimity, 2000), *Ratzinger studies* (The Theology of Pope Benedict XVI, 2010; O Lord, I Seek Your Countenance, 2018), *and Mariology. Father de Gaál has published in five languages and regularly delivers papers at international theological or philosophical conferences.*

Susan Benofy *received her doctorate in physics from Saint Louis University. She was formerly Research Editor of* Adoremus Bulletin.